REVISED AND EXPANDED

God's Word to Pastors

God's Word to Pastors

A PRACTICAL AND SPIRITUAL GUIDE
FOR EVERYDAY CHALLENGES IN MINISTRY

BOB YANDIAN

Published by Harrison House Publishers
Shippensburg, PA 17257

ISBN 13 TP: 978-1-6803-1855-5
ISBN 13 eBook: 978-1-6803-1856-2
ISBN 13 HC: 978-1-6803-1858-6
ISBN 13 LP: 978-1-6803-1857-9

For Worldwide Distribution, Printed in the U.S.A.
1 2 3 4 5 6 7 8 / 26 25 24 23 22

CONTENTS

INTRODUCTION

The pastor of the local church today has many voices crying out, from both the natural world and the Christian world. And as 1 Corinthians 14:10 tells us, *"...none of them is without significance."* Every voice is important.

As a former pastor, I know that books written by other pastors and ministers can bring great insight into the ministry and help us avoid some of the pitfalls. I also know that much can be learned from secular books on time management and business administration, books written by successful business executives.

Most Christians view the ministry as being all spiritual, but there are many practical aspects of ministry as well. Often we look to the Bible only for the spiritual side of ministry, and then seek out practical books on the natural side. But the Bible is still the best source of information for natural as well as spiritual living.

If a pastor were completely removed from all reading material except the Bible, the church could still be a great success, and the pastor's life could be balanced in both spiritual and natural areas.

Second Peter 1:3 says that God *"has given to us all things that pertain to life* [natural] *and godliness* [spiritual], *through the knowledge of Him...."* The same Bible that tells us how we are joined to the Lord Jesus Christ also tells us how to be successful in being joined together in marriage.

The Word of God tells us how to have a full relationship with our heavenly Father, but also gives principles to help us be successful parents. And not only does the Bible talk about faithfulness to God, it also deals with honoring your employer.

Because we are citizens of two worlds, the kingdom of God and planet Earth, the Holy Spirit was not slack in teaching us our responsibilities to each kingdom when He gave us the Word of God. He knows that ignorance of natural principles can lead to a spiritual disaster just as easily as ignorance of spiritual principles can lead to destruction in the natural.

When we face failure, we usually look for answers in fasting, longer prayer time, or possibly a promise we had overlooked or neglected to stand on from God's Word. But the problem could simply be a lack of time with our family or not delegating responsibility to others.

The *"little foxes that spoil the vines"* (Song of Solomon 2:15) are often overlooked as we strive to carry out the vision God has given us, but they are not overlooked in God's Word! Since the Lord created both worlds— spiritual and natural—He saw to it that His Word to us contained wisdom for both realms in our lives.

Acts 20:17-38 is one of those special passages for pastors, in which Paul shares the practical side of the ministry with the pastors of Ephesus. The man who wrote the great letter to the Ephesian congregation, teaching them their wonderful spiritual heritage, now sits with their pastors to share the realities of the everyday challenges of pastoring.

In 1 Peter 5:1-6, Peter's counsel to the pastors of scattered Jewish believers closely parallels the godly wisdom Paul imparts in Acts, chapter 20. Several other scriptures relate directly to how the pastor and the local church flow together in both spiritual things and natural things.

I'm certain that one of the main reasons the Holy Spirit included these passages of scripture in the Bible is that all ministers, but particularly pastors, are the favorite targets of Satan and his demon army. It is a great accomplishment for the devil to sidetrack a member of the congregation, but his greatest trophies are pastors he has managed to shipwreck.

Destruction of leadership leaves in its wake many more broken and confused followers. This is why the office of the pastor is always under such supernatural attack. If the enemy can eliminate the shepherd, he can scatter the flock and devour some of the sheep.

Discouragement, exhaustion, and frustration easily plague pastors if they don't recognize and follow certain natural principles in the Word of God. It doesn't take intense spiritual revelation to come out of many of the devil's traps.

Satan's devices can be as simple as causing ministers to get their priorities out of line or tempting them to value the wrong things at the wrong time. Also, pastors are often guilty of not heeding the wisdom in their own sermons!

By the time Paul and Peter imparted this practical wisdom to pastors, they had endured many years of ministry. They had learned what works and what doesn't, what to do and what not to do. And the principles they gave these ministers, if followed, will produce both longevity and joy in ministry for us today.

Chapter 1

PAUL CALLS THE FIRST PASTORS' CONFERENCE

From Miletus he sent to Ephesus and called for the elders of the church (Acts 20:17).

Paul was the apostle the Holy Spirit sent to establish the original church in Ephesus. He spent three years there, and during that time he experienced the most powerful revival of his ministry. From this great revival, many local churches were raised up, and many pastors were raised up with them.

A few months after leaving Ephesus, the Holy Spirit sent Paul back to minister to those same pastors. The very first pastors' conference is recorded in Acts 20:17-38 as Paul called for the pastors of Ephesus to join him in Miletus.

THE END RESULT OF REVIVAL

When Paul called the pastors of Ephesus to come to Miletus, they had been "in the trenches" for many months. After Paul's sudden and dramatic departure from them in Acts 19. If you remember, a riot led by the silver workers' union had broken out in Ephesus, and Paul was forced to flee for his life.

The revival lasted three years under Paul's apostleship, and left the silver industry—one of Ephesus' main industries—in economic disaster. Small figures of Diana, which usually brought great amounts of money from her worshippers, were now sitting on store shelves because people throughout Ephesus and the whole continent of Asia had turned to the Lord Jesus Christ.

Since the craft of these silver idols was a major industry in Ephesus, Demetrius, the president of the silver union, assembled a union meeting of all the craftsmen and put the blame for their financial losses on Paul's shoulders (Acts 19:24-27).

During the course of this assembly, a religious and patriotic frenzy mounted until it spread out into the streets with the emotional outcry, *"Great is Diana of the Ephesians!"* (Acts 19:28). Inevitably, the mob deteriorated into a confused group of people, yelling and rioting without really knowing why they were there.

Out of control, the angry crowd rushed the home of two innocent friends of Paul and dragged them into the center of town. Paul wanted to save them, but the other disciples begged him not to get involved (Acts 19:29-31).

Paul was caught in the middle of a divided city. His greatest desire was to stay with the new converts and help the new churches become established, but concern for his own safety overruled his desire, and with an emotional departure, he left for Macedonia (Acts 20:1).

After Paul's departure, the new churches had to stand on their own as the explosive situation in Ephesus continued. Months later, when Paul returned and asked them to meet him in Miletus (Acts 20:17), they were ready for some encouragement!

These pastors and ministers must have felt orphaned when Paul was rushed out of town during the riot at Ephesus. More importantly, their minds must have raced with questions, "Is this the result of revival in a city? Does God bring a man like Paul here only to have him run out of town? And if God brings revival, can men end it? How can something begin in such power and end in such confusion?"

No doubt, pastors' congregations were also asking many of these questions:

- "Where are the miracles now? Will we ever see special miracles like Paul's when handkerchiefs and aprons from ministers cause disease and evil spirits to leave the sick and oppressed?" (Acts 19:11-12).

- "Will more of Satan's ministers be exposed, like the seven sons of Sceva?" (Acts 19:13-17).

- "Will we see more followers of the occult burn their books publicly as they acknowledge Jesus as their Lord and Savior?" (Acts 19:19).

Believers today are asking the same questions:

- "Will we see another Azusa Street, healing movements, charismatic revival, Billy Graham or Oral Roberts?"

- "Will tremendous healings and miracles be front-page news again?"

- "Will denominational barriers crumble under the powerful move of the Holy Spirit as they did in the charismatic movement?"

Believers today are crying out for more revival, but is the conclusion of revival more revival? The answer is simple and obvious as we study the aftermath of the revival in Ephesus in Acts, chapter 20. The result of the revival was the establishing of local churches that turned their communities "right side up" (Acts 17:6).

Nowhere in the Bible is there an example of perpetual revival. Revival produces many converts filled with zeal, but stability comes from growing up spiritually within the local church. Remember that our command was not to make *converts* of all nations, but *disciples* (Matthew 28:19-20).

A *disciple*, defined by Jesus in John 8:31-32, is one who continues in God's Word. This definition is confirmed in the account of the Ephesus revival in Acts, chapter 19. After the mass conversions, miracles, healings, exposing of false ministers, and burning of occult literature, verse 20 states, *"So the word of the Lord grew mightily and prevailed."*

After revival, Ephesus had a "Word" movement. Local churches were springing up to make disciples of converts by teaching the Word of God. Revival is successful only through the growth of local assemblies where the teaching of the Word of God brings stability to the congregation.

Ephesus was divided by the gospel but stabilized by the local church. The church of Ephesus went on to be one of the greatest of the ancient world. After the church at Jerusalem fell into legalism, and Antioch had periods of legalism, the church of Ephesus became the main center of world evangelism.

Timothy pastored the church of Ephesus during Paul's second imprisonment; therefore, Ephesus was the recipient of both of Paul's letters to Timothy. This church also became one of the largest in the ancient world, numbering in the tens of thousands.

The gospel shook Ephesus and Asia, but the church of Ephesus shook the world with the gospel!

WHAT ABOUT AMERICA?

In our own country, we have seen a tremendous hunger for the Word of God after the healing movement of the 1950s and the charismatic movement of the 1960s. Hunger for the Word of God causes the transition from revival to the birth of local churches.

Today, strong local churches are being established around the world; and as pastors preach and teach the Word of God to their people, these believers are transforming their communities.

Many of these churches have weekly crowds that outnumber the tent meetings and seminars of years ago. The hunger for God and His Word is being satisfied, and the needs of the people are being supernaturally met in the local church today.

As revival moved across the nation in tents and seminars during the healing and charismatic movements, God began to raise up pastors who proclaimed, "Why should people have to go to a special meeting to hear the Word of God to be healed or to have their family restored? These blessings should be found in the local church!"

The Bible does not say, "Is there any sick among you, let him call for the elders of the tent or the seminar." There should be elders of the local church who know how to pray for healing (James 5:14).

Just like the church of Ephesus, the local church is ordained to be the focal point of evangelism into its community, and a hub of evangelism into the world as they support missionaries whom God raises up in their midst.

The other full-time ministry offices of apostles, prophets, evangelists, and teachers should also be members of a local church along with their families. A traveling ministry is stabilized when they have a home church praying for them and supporting them. It is not an accident that the time we live in is called the church age!

The local church is the visible, living example of the invisible universal Church, and Jesus said, *"the gates of Hades shall not prevail against it"* (Matthew 16:18). While movements, ministries, and revivals come and go, the local church continues to survive. I believe local churches will be victorious and triumphant monuments to the power of God when Jesus returns.

PASTORS NEED PASTORING TOO

Pastors teach, uplift, and encourage their congregations day after day, service after service, and week after week, but who encourages them? They have their treasure in an earthen vessel just like all other Christians, and with time their vessel can become tired, discouraged, and even disoriented.

There are times when a pastor needs to get away to be pastored himself, just like those from Ephesus. That is why it is good to attend pastors' conferences.

For those of you who are going into the ministry or are already in the ministry, it is good to occasionally take a break from the church, sit down with other pastors and discover that your problems are not unique—that you are not the only one facing difficult situations.

I want you to note, although Paul's conference was for the pastors at Ephesus, the conference was not held there, it was held in Miletus, a small town about thirty miles south of Ephesus. Besides the continued danger to his life in Ephesus, there is another reason why God had Paul call these pastors away from their churches to meet with him.

Whenever there is a pastors' conference in my hometown where I pastor, I rarely attend. The conferences I usually participate in are out of town because I have no pressure to be at the church.

When I go to a conference away from home, I can attend the entire meeting and hear all the speakers. I can give my full attention to receiving from God. The wisdom of God led Paul to bring the pastors of Ephesus away from their homes and their churches. In this way, they could truly rest from the challenges of the ministry, attend all the meetings of the conference, and get a fresh perspective as they enjoyed the company of other ministers.

What Paul shared with these pastors in the town of Miletus is as powerful and effective for us today as it was for the Ephesian pastors in the early days of the church age. Problems have not changed, because Satan and his demons are still the same. Nor have the answers changed, because *"Jesus Christ is the same yesterday, today, and forever"* (Hebrews 13:8).

Chapter 2

HOLD NOTHING BACK

And when they had come to him, he said to them: "You know, from the first day that I came to Asia, in what manner I always lived among you, serving the Lord with all humility, with many tears and trials which happened to me by the plotting of the Jews; how I kept back nothing that was helpful, but proclaimed it to you, and taught you publicly and from house to house" (Acts 20:18-20).

These three verses of scripture in Acts 20 begin Paul's message to the elders of Ephesus. He had come to give them encouragement and instruction, to pour out all the knowledge and wisdom he could to help them accomplish what God has called them to do.

As an apostle, Paul had also functioned as pastor of the first church that began in Ephesus, and many of these pastors had come up directly under his leadership.

The Holy Spirit may lead an apostle to start a church, and while the apostle temporarily serves as pastor to that church, God will often raise up the pastor from among the elders. The apostle will then move on to begin another church, and the process begins again.

That is what Paul had done with many of these men. For the moment, Paul was speaking to them as a pastor to pastors—as the apostle who had helped them grow up in the ministry—a spiritual father to his sons.

AT ALL SEASONS

Paul began by saying, *"...You know, from the first day that I came to Asia, in what manner I always lived among you."* This time refers to the three years Paul had spent with the elders. They had seen him at his best, and they had seen him at his worst!

This should remind us that our lives have times of rejoicing and times of sorrow, times of excitement and times of boredom, times of frustration and times of contentment. Just as the year brings different seasons, our lives undergo many changes. The only One who never changes is Jesus (Hebrews 13:8).

Therefore, Paul instructed pastors to be transparent with their people. He exhorted them to admit when they had made mistakes, and praise God and give Him glory in their victories. Paul encouraged pastors to tell their people that they faced difficult seasons in their lives just as their congregations did.

As pastors are faithful in the Word of God, their congregations will see consistency in their lives. No one is on top of it every single day. So, don't kid yourself.

The point is, there are times when you are up and there are times when you are down, so don't give the impression that you are always up. If you do, you will discourage your people.

If the pastor is always "up there," the congregation will think they can never arrive at his level. Jesus was tempted in all points as we are (Hebrews 4:15). Even though He did not sin, He still experienced everything you and I experience. Because of this, He can say to us, "I was right there too, and I'll strengthen you to make it through this ordeal successfully."

Paul was saying to these pastors, "There were times when I came to preach to you, and I was really inspired. There were times when there was no inspiration and there were other times when I was discouraged and upset.

"Pressures were on me from religious or government leaders. Money was tight. But I'll tell you what, you saw me *at all seasons*. And I continued to preach and teach the Word regardless of what was going on in my life. I was as genuine out of the pulpit as I was in the pulpit. I remained faithful."

Stay faithful! That is one of the keys of the kingdom of God—faithfulness. Paul was making the point that he lived a consistent life before the pastors. He reminded these pastors that God does not reward you for staying "on top." He rewards you for being faithful, for being consistent in the Word of God, and in your lifestyle before others.

In Philippians 3:13-14 Paul wrote, *"Brethren, I do not count myself to have apprehended; but one thing I do, forgetting those things which are behind and reaching forward to those things which are ahead, I press toward the goal for the prize of the upward call of God in Christ Jesus."*

It is good to let your congregation know you haven't arrived yet. But, in the face of every situation and every circumstance, whether good or bad, whether up or down, you show yourself to be faithful in all seasons to study and teach them the Word of God.

GRACE THINKING

Paul continued in Acts 20:18-19 with, *"You know, from the first day that I came to Asia, in what manner I always lived among you, serving the Lord with all humility...."* You may ask, "What does he mean *'with all humility'*?" I call this "grace thinking."

"Grace thinking" is getting rid of all thoughts of superiority. It is humbling yourself before God and seeing others the way He sees them.

There are always going to be people who irritate and frustrate you as you minister and counsel them. If you choose the attitude of *"Serving the Lord with all humility of mind"* (Acts 20:19 KJV), or "grace thinking," you will obtain the grace from God that enables you to continue to minister to them effectively and compassionately. But if you decide you are better than they are, you will grow more and more impatient and insensitive to them. The Bible says to serve the Lord with *"all humility,"* or "grace thinking."

It is so important that, as a minister, you look at your people through the eyes of grace—through the eyes of love. It is easy to become discouraged with people when they come back for spiritual help more than once for the same problem or ask you the same questions time after time.

It is very easy to look at a person who is struggling over simple issues and think, "How stupid!"

Now don't think I haven't been tempted in this way! I'm human. There are times when people would come into my office and I would think, "Don't you know what the Word says?" It seems to me they are overlooking one of the simplest verses in the Bible. But when "grace thinking" is working in my life, the Lord says, "How long did it take YOU to learn that?" Then I would see them through the eyes of His compassion.

How long did He have to put up with *me* in certain areas? How long did it take *me* to learn certain lessons? How many times did God have to pick *me* up for the same stupid mistake I kept committing? Oh, how quickly we forget our own weaknesses, yet we demand perfection of everyone around us.

Paul was exhorting the pastors to look at their congregations through the same eyes of grace and love through which the Lord Jesus Christ viewed them, to treat their people as Jesus treated them. Pastors need to remember that God's Word and patience are what changed them, and it took time!

WITH MANY TEARS

There are times in the ministry when you will experience hurt, pain, and the shedding of tears. In fact, Paul told his friends he was *"Serving the Lord with all humility of mind, and **with many tears**"* (Acts 20:19 KJV).

You ask, "Why do tears come?" Very often, it is because you learn what people are *really* like. People often wear facades when they come to church. They have big smiles on their faces, and they make great promises about what they are going to do for you—then you never hear from them again.

On other occasions people will say, "I will pledge toward the building program. Do you need some chairs? I'll buy twenty of them!" So, you think "Glory to God!" Then you see them the next week, and you think, *What about the pledge? What about the chairs?* And they just walk by, smile, and never keep the commitment they made to you.

That is when you have to catch yourself, "No! I can't think that way!" You cannot look at people through the eyes of their promises. You may find out that what they promised was something they wanted to do, but in the end was beyond their ability to accomplish.

You learn very quickly in the ministry that presumptuous talk is common within the local church. You learn to take promises with a grain of salt. If they promise, don't immediately get excited. Let them prove themselves.

New people will walk in and tell you yours is the church they have been looking for. They tell you they will be back next week to join, and then you never see them again. Others will tell you when you first take over the church that you are the pastor they have been praying for. They will commit to help in any area you need them, attend for two or three weeks, and never return!

Ironically, one of the most difficult times for the pastor is when the church begins to grow. Church growth is a blessing, but more blessing brings more responsibility and more problems. The most common complaints are, "Things aren't like they used to be. I used to know everyone. Now it seems so cold. Pastor used to come pray for me, but now he sends one of his workers."

Many members cannot handle the change from a smaller building to a larger one. When people are crowded into a sanctuary, sitting in the aisles and standing around the back, the excitement of a big crowd can be mistaken for powerful anointing!

When you move into a new larger facility, suddenly there are empty seats. The pastor begins to hear, "There is no anointing in this building. The church has really changed since we moved. Church is just not as exciting and powerful as it used to be."

Another hurt comes when faithful people leave the church. Their family was saved, and they were faithful to the Word of God. You saw their lives turn around as they grew weekly in the Word. Their appearance changed and they became happier and healthier. Then one day they were no longer sitting in the service.

After several Sundays pass and they have not returned, you call them and ask how they are doing and why they haven't been to church. They reply, "The church has just grown too big, Pastor." We are going to a smaller church where we can really feel a part of things." Later, you hear about them having serious problems again because although the church they have been attending is smaller, the Word is not being taught, believed, or practiced.

As the church grows, the pastor has less one-on-one contact with the members. Because he cannot and should not do everything himself, he begins to delegate his authority in various areas to others. This offends some people, even if he teaches the principle of delegation from the Word of God (see Chapter 5).

They refuse to believe God can use anyone other than the pastor to pray for their need. So, they leave the church saying, "The pastor has just gotten too big to minister to us." In reality, the church has gotten too big for the pastor to minister to them personally. Even though he has provided someone on staff or a capable volunteer to pray for their needs, they are not satisfied because it is not the pastor.

It is ironic that a congregation will pray to reach their city for Jesus, that people will come and be saved, and when the church does grow, they leave! However, the strain of church growth on a congregation is as old as the Church. In Acts 6:1 it says, *"Now in those days, when the number of the disciples was multiplying, there arose a complaint...."*

To appease those who were complaining, the apostles appointed deacons to minister to the people so they could concentrate on the Word of God and prayer (the pastor's primary responsibilities). The murmurers were probably some of those who had been shouting for joy in the upper room a few months before!

These are the *"many tears"* from *within* the church, but there are also tears from outside the church. Paul refers to these tears when he writes: *"serving the Lord with all humility, with many tears and trials which happened to me by the plotting of the Jews"* (Acts 20:19).

The worst enemy to the gospel has always been and always will be religion. Because so many people think that faith in Jesus Christ is "religion," I want to define this term before going any further.

"Religion" is any counterfeit of or alternative to salvation and Christian living through faith in Jesus Christ. True Christianity is not religion; it is an intimate relationship between God and man. Religion, on the other hand, is a system of rules and traditions that, if kept by its followers, will supposedly cause them to gain acceptance with God. But religion can never bring man into a relationship with God.

When Paul said, *"the plotting of the Jews,"* he literally meant the religious Jews who had plotted against him, trying to destroy his reputation and ministry, even attempting to take his life. They were violently opposed to the teachings of faith and grace Paul preached, looking to the law and Jewish tradition for salvation and daily living.

Some of the biggest opposition a pastor confronts will not be from the world—it will be from the churches around town. But recall that Jesus' biggest problem during His public ministry was from religious Jews, not the sinner on the street.

Problems can come from another denomination or from your same persuasion. Much of it comes from jealousy. Some of the members of their church left to go to yours. They start gossip about you and run you down, picking anything they can find that is wrong with you or your church. In essence, they feel like all the churches in town are competing.

One of the most destructive beliefs a pastor can have is that he has a monopoly on his city. If someone else starts a church in his town, somehow he feels that the new pastor should check with him first. After all, he believes,

"I am a founding pastor in this city, and no one should come to start a church unless I give my approval first!"

That is the first indication you are headed downhill. God will lift the anointing right off of your church. He will find somebody else who will walk in love toward the other churches—regardless of what they say or do. God is not concerned with establishing or building your reputation; He is in the business of saving people and stabilizing them in His Word.

If God has called you to begin a work in a city—especially if it is in a smaller town—I would advise you to let the other pastors in the city know. This is only proper; it is just good manners. By showing respect for the leaders who are already established in a city, you might avoid many problems later.

Here is another scenario I have seen. One pastor starts a church and plods away for years to get a few hundred members. Then another pastor starts a church across town, and the thing explodes. What took the first pastor years to accomplish the other does in a matter of months. The first pastor then becomes jealous and begins to run down the new pastor and his church. In the end, he hurts his own church members.

In the city where I was pastor, it was common for new churches to spring up. Often, we would lose some of our members as God called them to another church, but I would tell them, "If God wants you there, go!"

One of the greatest joys to me was when people would say, "Pastor Bob, there is a little church starting across town, with just twenty or thirty members. We visited last week, and God told us we are supposed to attend there and help them."

"Praise God!" I tell them, "We'll miss you, but go! If God called you there, you would get stagnant if you stayed here."

There were also times when someone would come up after a service and say, "Pastor Bob, we've been to a church across town and today God spoke to us that this is where He wants us to be, so we would like to become members of your church today." In these moments, I would be reminded *"the Lord added to the church daily those who were being saved"* (Acts 2:47).

Pastors and churches should not feel threatened by each other. We are all branch offices working for the same Boss! I am thoroughly convinced if your entire city were saved, every church in town would be packed out. We don't have to steal sheep; we can go out and turn goats into sheep any day!

I should mention there are times when one of your sheep will come to you and say they are leaving, and you know something is wrong. This is when you leave the ninety-nine and go after the one. You find out what the problem is and minister to them. The sheep that go astray from the flock, fall into the crevice, and need to be lifted out and brought back to the fold are the ones you need to pursue.

Other times a member of the congregation will tell you they are leaving, and you know their decision is not right. But when you go after them and minister to them, they turn up their tail and keep going. In such cases, let them go! Once you have talked to them two or three times, if they are still angry, what can you do?

When this occurred at our church, I asked the Lord what I should do, and He gave me some great wisdom. He said, "The one you go after is the one who trips and falls, not the one who turns up their tail and just leaves. You have better things to do than go after a sheep who will not turn. Kick the dust off your feet and go on with what I've called you to do."

Some pastors are running from person to person, trying to soothe their feelings and bring understanding. If you do not use wisdom regarding this, it can become a waste of time. Life is too short to chase people who are angry, mad, or upset after you have done all you can. Leave them in the Lord's hands and forget it.

It comes down to this: Do what God has called you and your church to do, regardless of what the church or pastor down the street does.

Pray for the churches in your town to prosper in the things of God and walk in love toward them and their pastors. Most importantly, do not defend yourself. Just keep teaching the Word of God, obeying the Holy Spirit, and let God defend you. Remember, *"When a man's ways please the Lord, he makes even his enemies to be at peace with him"* (Proverbs 16:7).

DON'T FURL THE SAILS

In Acts 20:20, Paul continued, *"how I kept back nothing that was helpful, but proclaimed it to you, and taught you publicly and from house to house."* Here, Paul used a very picturesque Greek word for *"kept back nothing."* It is the word *hupostello*.

Hupostello paints a picture of a sailing vessel on which none of the sails are furled or tied back. When a sailor wants to lessen the speed at which a ship is sailing, they furl the sails, or fold the sails back to where very little of the face of the sail is catching the wind.

But Paul wanted this ship—the local church—to go full speed ahead, as fast as the wind would carry it. The captain of this ship—the pastor—is not to fold back or "furl" any of the sails to try to hinder or slow down the ship as it travels toward its destination.

Literally Paul was saying, "Do not furl the sails in the ministry. Whatever God has given you, whatever the Chief Shepherd has fed you, you feed that to the sheep—hold nothing back."

Sometimes when ministers teach or preach to other ministers, they might be tempted to withhold some of the revelation God has given them in order to "corner the market" on a particular subject or issue. But Paul was commanding these pastors to share everything with their elders, bishops, and deacons, as well as their congregations.

Also, while you are ministering the Word of God to the people, many things come to you by the Holy Spirit. Sometimes I will receive revelation while I'm in the pulpit. Verses of scripture will rise up that I hadn't thought of using, or I might feel led of the Spirit to veer from the main topic for a few minutes. However, these "rabbit trails" directly relate to what I'm saying. There may only be one person or a portion of the congregation who needed to hear it. The Holy Spirit may even have me take a major detour just to set somebody free in a certain area.

Let me make one distinction. Paul is talking to pastors and elders of the local churches, who function very differently from someone who stands in the fivefold ministry office of the prophet (Ephesians 4:11).

There are times when a prophet of God may be restrained by the Holy Spirit from telling the people everything that has been revealed to him simply because it is not the right time to reveal it. I have heard some genuine, proven prophets say, "God showed me this fifteen years ago, and He says the time has come to let you know," and it was exactly what the people needed at that time.

However, a pastor cannot function this way. He cannot "furl the sail" or hold anything back from the people. When God shows something to him from the

Word, he must give his congregation everything he has. *He cannot withhold grass from the sheep.*

THE PROOF OF THE MINISTRY

How I kept back nothing that was helpful, but proclaimed it to you, and taught you publicly and from house to house (Acts 20:20).

When he first came to Ephesus, Paul not only taught in the synagogue, he taught publicly in the school of Tyrannus, and in various homes of the people (see Acts 19:1-10). When Paul says he *showed* them the gospel along with teaching it, this simply means he lived it before them.

Paul trained these pastors. Many of them were his apprentices, some of them traveled with him, and many of them took churches Paul had begun as an apostle. They were right there at his side when he preached the gospel and they saw many saved, miraculously healed, and set free.

The words *"proclaimed it to you"* and *"taught you"* are very important here, because ministry is not all preaching and teaching. Ministry is also *"accompanying signs"* (Mark 16:20). The gospel is not only preached, but also demonstrated:

"And these signs will follow those who believe: In My name they will cast out demons; they will speak with new tongues; they will take up

serpents; and if they drink anything deadly, it will by no means hurt them; they will lay hands on the sick, and they will recover." So then, after the Lord had spoken to them, He was received up into heaven, and sat down at the right hand of God. And they went out and preached everywhere, the Lord working with them and confirming the word through the accompanying signs (Mark 16:17-20).

Some people are born again when they hear the gospel preached; they hear the Word of God and receive it. Others are saved when they see a great miracle or healing, which is a sign and a wonder. Signs and wonders cause the fear of God to fall on people and receive Jesus as Lord and Savior.

For I will not dare to speak of any of those things which Christ has not accomplished through me, in word and deed, to make the Gentiles [heathen] obedient—in mighty signs and wonders, by the power of the Spirit of God, so that from Jerusalem and round about to Illyricum I have fully preached the gospel of Christ (Romans 15:18-19).

You may be asking what it means *"to make the Gentiles obedient."* The Gentiles who are unbelievers become "obedient" believers when they receive Jesus as their Lord.

They were formerly in rebellion with Satan, but now they are in obedience to God through Jesus Christ.

And how are they made obedient? The scripture goes on to say how: *"...in word and deed!"* In other words, the Gentiles become obedient—receive salvation—by the preaching of the Word of God, with signs and wonders following.

When Paul says, *"word and deed,"* he is stressing the fact that both God's Word and the power of the Holy Spirit are involved in the preaching of the Gospel. God's Word and power must always be in balance in our lives. We never dismiss one for the other, and where we have one, we should have the other.

There have been times in history when not one word was spoken, yet the hand of God was in demonstration to the point that people would fall on their faces and accept Jesus as their Savior. However, these new believers then needed the *"pure milk of the word"* that they *"may grow thereby"* (1 Peter 2:2). So even in these unusual moves of God, the Spirit and the Word will both be present.

You can preach for hours, one sermon after another, and pat yourself on the back—but there must be more than this. Let God be God! Preach His Word; and when your preaching ends, stand back and allow His power to break forth. Then you will begin to understand that it is not by your eloquence or your great knowledge or abilities that people are saved, healed, and delivered, but by the Spirit of God. Paul speaks of this in 1 Corinthians:

And my speech and my preaching were not with persuasive words of human wisdom, but in demonstration of the Spirit and of power, that your faith should not be in the wisdom of men but in the power of God (1 Corinthians 2:4-5).

Paul taught openly in fields, on the streets, and from house to house. In those days, many churches met in houses. Many of these pastors and elders were saved in the field or on the streets—but as believers, they would fellowship together in homes.

In light of this, Paul exhorted them, "Remember my example. Don't furl the sails. Preach the Word with power wherever the Holy Spirit leads. Hold nothing back!"

Chapter 3

BOUND IN THE SPIRIT

Testifying both to Jews, and also to Greeks, repentance toward God and faith toward our Lord Jesus Christ. And see, now I go bound in the spirit to Jerusalem, not knowing the things that will happen to me there, except that the Holy Spirit testifies in every city, saying that chains and tribulations await me. But none of these things move me; nor do I count my life dear to myself, so that I may finish my race with joy, and the ministry which I have received from the Lord Jesus, to testify to the gospel of the grace of God (Acts 20:21-24).

In Acts 20:21, Paul states he testified both *"to Jews and also to Greeks."* It was important for Paul to share this with the pastors because the gospel is for everyone. Paul was reminding them of that fact. God has never excluded anyone from being saved because of race, color, nationality, gender, or how they dress or wear their hair.

Romans 1:16 says the gospel is *"the power of God to salvation to everyone who believes, for the Jew first, and also for the Greek."* The gospel was preached first to the Jew, then to the Gentile. The Gospel is all-inclusive.

In the Old Testament, we see where God gave the plan of salvation to the nation of Israel through the teaching of the law and the sacrifices. It was then their responsibility to take it to all the nations of the world. As an example of this, God told Jonah to go to Nineveh, a Gentile city, and preach (Jonah 3:1-2).

There are great examples of Gentile revivals in the Old Testament. Some of these Gentile believers, such as Ruth and Rahab, were even added to the genealogical line that brought forth Jesus Christ (Matthew 1; Luke 3).

But Israel failed to carry out God's will. By the time Jesus came into the world, the Jews had become so entrenched in the religious rites and rituals and consumed with the letter of the law instead of the Spirit of the law, they did not even recognize their own Messiah, Jesus of Nazareth.

That is the reason Jesus said to them in Matthew 21:43, *"Therefore say I to you, the kingdom of God will be taken from you, and given to a nation bearing the fruits of it."*

In this verse, Jesus was correctly prophesying that the gospel was being preached first to the Jew. However, most in the Jewish nation would ultimately reject Him as their Messiah. Jesus was prophesying about the church age.

PAUL'S CALLING

When Paul says, *"Testifying both to Jews, and also to Greeks,"* he is referring to the fact that he himself has preached and taught in synagogues to the Jew and on the streets to the Gentile, just as Jesus had. However, the book of Acts makes it clear that Paul was called *first* to the Gentiles.

Jesus revealed Paul's calling in Acts 9:15 when He said to Ananias, *"Go, for he* [Paul] *is a chosen vessel of Mine to bear My name before Gentiles, kings, and the children of Israel."*

Notice, Paul is to bear the name of Jesus *first* to the Gentiles, *then* before kings, and *lastly* to the Jew. But in Acts 20:21, Paul reverses the order! He mentions first that he testified to the Jew and then to the Gentile (Greek).

You will see why this is important in verse 22. This is one indication that Paul's priorities were out of order and that he is about to step out of God's will.

PAUL'S PASSION

In Acts 20:22, Paul told the pastors of Ephesus that he planned to go to Jerusalem, despite a check in his spirit and repeated warnings from the Holy Spirit. He said, *"And see, now I go **bound in the spirit** to Jerusalem...."*

Paul's spirit, by the Holy Spirit, was telling him not to go to Jerusalem, but in the next verses he rationalizes the "no" he senses in his spirit, into a "yes." Have you ever done that? God is telling you one thing, and you just rationalize it into something else. Your desires try to reshape God's will.

Paul's calling was first to the Gentiles (Acts 9:15; Galatians 2:7), but in Acts 20:21, he mentions his testimony *"to the Jew first, and also to the Greeks."* Paul is working against his calling because of his personal desire to see the church at Jerusalem, comprised of Jewish believers, return to the grace of God and turn from the legalistic bondage into which they had fallen.

Notice too that Paul was suddenly in a hurry. Acts 20:16 says, *"For Paul had decided to sail past Ephesus, so that he would not have to spend time in Asia; for* he was hurrying *to be at Jerusalem, if possible, on the Day of Pentecost."*

One indicator you could be missing God's will is when you are being pressured by time. Often the devil will pressure you to act immediately or impulsively making you believe you will be missing the will of God if you don't act *now*. It is not characteristic of the Holy Spirit to tell you to do something new or to make a major change the day before you are to do it. He gives you ample time to question Him and wait on Him to confirm that it is His will.

It seems clear that the Holy Spirit was doing all He could to get through to Paul: *"...not knowing the things that will happen to me there, except that the Holy Spirit testifies in every city, saying that chains and tribulations await me"* (Acts 20:22-23).

From the moment Paul made up his mind to go to Jerusalem, wherever he went Christians would say, "Paul, you are not supposed to go to Jerusalem. You are going to be bound and thrown into prison."

I can just imagine that as he went from city to city and town to town, people would stop him and say, "The Holy Spirit told me to tell you not to go to Jerusalem."

This is one example the Bible gives about how the Holy Spirit will speak to you through other believers. It is usually a person who does not know anything about you. They tell you what you already know in your heart. In other words, the Holy Spirit will use an outside source to confirm what He has already shown you inwardly.

Paul knew in his own spirit—*"bound in his spirit"*—that he was not to go to Jerusalem. In the following verse, he mentioned that everywhere he went the Holy Spirit had been using other believers to tell him the same thing.

However, in verse 24 Paul says, *"But none of these things move me...."* What is Paul saying? He is still determined to do what *he* wants to do. The rest of this verse reveals just how determined Paul was: *"...nor do I count my life dear to myself, so that I might finish my race with joy, and the ministry which I received from the Lord Jesus, to testify the gospel of the grace of God."*

Everything Paul is saying sounds right, but his attitude was wrong, and he was traveling to the wrong location. He was noble but stupid! You can have the right messages, preach and teach the Word of God, but nothing will be accomplished by your efforts if your desires are not in line with God's desires.

Pastors have told me, "I've been at this church so long and nothing has worked out. I've preached and taught the Word, and when I study and prepare, the anointing is so strong. And yet, when I get up in the pulpit, I'm doing and saying the right things but there is no anointing. I am miserable!"

I will often ask them some basic questions, "Are you in God's will? Are you sure you're supposed to pastor? If you are certain you are called to pastor, are you called to this church?" In most cases, the answer is either no or the pastor is confused and uncertain.

When Paul said, "I don't even count my life dear to myself, even if I have to die while I'm here," it sounds commendable. But why die out of God's will? Why give your life unnecessarily?

Paul took what the Holy Spirit and his spirit were saying that afflictions and imprisonment would await him if he went to Jerusalem, and he turned a type of self-imposed persecution into the will of God.

How often have you heard someone say, "Well, if I am being persecuted, it must be the will of God"? But you can also be persecuted because you are out of the will of God. Peter tells us it is fine to accept buffeting when you are in the will of God, but what glory is there when you are persecuted for your faults (1 Peter 2:20)?

The Holy Spirit had not only witnessed to Paul in every city, but in Acts 21, he was stopped on four specific occasions by people warning him not to go to Jerusalem, all in reference to the same event. Agabus, a prophet of God, told Paul not to go. Then, his own team members also told him not to go (Acts 21:1-12).

Nevertheless, Paul continued to *"testify the gospel of the grace of God."* Again, it seems there could be nothing better than to walk into a legalistic place like Jerusalem and preach grace to them. Sounds great, doesn't it? But why is the Holy Spirit trying to stop Paul?

The Holy Spirit knew Paul could go to Jerusalem and preach grace under a strong anointing and yet, no one would accept him or the message. Even more, the Holy Spirit knew when Paul did try to preach grace to them, they would try to kill him. In other words, the Holy Spirit knew the Jewish believers in Jerusalem had hardened their hearts by choosing to live by the law instead of the Spirit. He knew it was not only a waste of time for Paul to go there, but it was also dangerous.

When Paul arrived at Jerusalem, the elders would not allow him to preach until he had taken a legalistic vow (Acts 21:22-24). Paul agreed to shave his head and fast for seven days according to an old religious, traditional vow, just so he could preach grace!

Paul would contradict his own teaching: *"Shall we continue in sin that grace may abound? Certainly not!"* (Romans 6:1-2).

Can you see that Paul had compromised the message of grace in order to preach it? He was talking about preaching grace in Jerusalem, but he did not practice grace when he arrived.

When the Word of God is compromised as a means to an end, what was intended to be kept will be lost. Even before Paul's seven-day cleansing was complete, the Jews tried to kill him. He never preached grace to them at all. If the Roman soldiers had not intervened, Paul would have been killed.

PASSION VERSUS CALLING

Never put passion above principle. You may think you are right, but you are wrong. One trap I see the devil set for ministers is illustrated here in Acts, chapters 20 and 21. Paul made the decision to go to Jerusalem. Rather than continue ministering the gospel to the Gentiles, as God had called him to do, Paul was determined to minister to the Jews.

Everyone has certain issues about which they are passionate. Paul's passion was his own people, the Jews. Romans 9:3 says, *"For I could wish that I myself were accursed from Christ for my brethren, my countrymen according to the flesh."*

Paul was so passionate about the Jews coming to Christ, he said if it were possible, he would give up his own salvation for theirs. With the situation in the Jerusalem church, the strong emotions Paul had for his people was joined by the passion he had for the doctrine he preached so strongly—the grace of God.

It had been approximately five years since Paul had been to Jerusalem and he was probably appalled at the apostasy that existed among the Jewish believers. Legalism had so crept into the church that they were not even preaching the gospel. Instead, they were preaching the law.

The elders were preaching circumcision for salvation, and teaching Old Testament rules and regulations for the Christian life. It grieved Paul's heart that the law was being taught as the means of spirituality instead of God's grace.

Up to the time of the pastor's conference in Miletus, the Holy Spirit had used Paul twice to go to Jerusalem and reestablish the gospel of grace among the Jewish believers there. After Paul left, the legalistic Jews began to preach the law again and the church slipped further into bondage than before.

Now when the Holy Spirit was directing him to call a meeting of the pastors of Ephesus, Paul was once again overcome with his passion for his Jewish brethren in Jerusalem who had fallen into spiritual bondage to the law once more. So he willfully disobeyed the direction of the Holy Spirit, and stepped out of God's will, allowing his feelings about a serious issue interfere with what God had called him to do.

Because Paul avoided the Lord's warning when he arrived in Jerusalem, his own actions removed God's protection and divine keeping power. He was almost beaten to death by the Jews, without uttering one word of the gospel. Paul's life was spared only because the Roman law and government stepped in.

We must carefully guard our hearts and make certain the works we are doing are what we have been called to do and not something that moves us emotionally. Remember, Satan will try to use our passions to distract and deceive us away from our calling.

There are many legitimate issues and areas of need that the body of Christ should be involved in, but that is why we are "the body" and not just one member. Seek God about what He has called you to and do it with all of your heart and might.

Not only is this true for churches, it is also true for individuals. Some churches have a vision for teaching, others are led to concentrate on missions, while others are called to evangelize their city. Churches are as different and unique as the pastors who lead them.

If you, as a congregational member, have strong feelings about a certain area of ministry, talk to your pastor, but do not become upset if he does not share your enthusiasm. Just like Paul, you may have a consuming passion for something, but it may not be God's will for your particular church.

Many members of my congregation were involved in and consumed with various important issues such as abortion, pornography, homosexuality, child abuse, or the homeless. As a pastor, I could let these areas overwhelm me and get myself and the church over-involved in these legitimate issues. I too could be noble, but stupid!

That is why it is vital for the pastor to stay in prayer and continuous study of the Word so he can be certain of God's vision for his particular church and be determined to fulfill it. Second Peter 1:10 says through the study of the Word of God you will be *"diligent to make your call and election sure."*

If you have strong feelings in a certain area, pray and ask God if it is His will for you or your church to become actively involved with it. Check yourself and make certain you are maintaining enough time in the Word to stay balanced.

If it becomes clear it is not God's will for you or your church to become involved, continue interceding for those who are called to be there. In this way, you can avoid wasting time, or even falling into destructive situations by getting out of God's will.

MINISTERS MAKE MISTAKES

It is encouraging to know even a great man of God like Paul erred. Ministers are human. They make mistakes, they sin, and they prove themselves to be human just like everyone else.

I repeatedly told my congregation that I am anointed to teach the Word of God, but I am *not* anointed to live it. I have to walk out my faith minute-by-minute, hour-by-hour, and day-by-day just like they do.

Even though Paul made a mistake, as recounted in the book of Acts, God still managed to bring him before kings, Agrippa and Caesar, and before Gentile leaders. Even when we sin, if we repent, God still has a plan for our life.

It is very important to understand when you go against God's will, it will *always* cost you something. In this case, Paul's actions cost him several years.

I am not saying it is acceptable to "sin now and repent later." What I am saying is, *"My little children, these things I write to you, so that you may not sin. And if anyone sins, we have an Advocate with the Father, Jesus Christ the righteous"* (1 John 2:1).

I am also saying, *"If we confess our sins, He is faithful and just to forgive us our sins and to cleanse us from all unrighteousness"* (1 John 1:9).

As I travel across the country, I meet so many ministers who are no longer in the ministry because they sinned and feel like they can no longer fulfill God's call on their lives. This is a great tragedy.

There are cities and towns crying out for pastors and teachers while many called to the ministry are driving taxicabs or waiting tables in total defeat. If that is you, I encourage you to follow the apostle Paul's example. Repent, pick yourself up, dust yourself off, and get back to God's will for your life.

You can take a test to determine if God is finished with your life: *Put your hand over your heart and if it is still beating, God is not through with you!* Go out and do what God tells you to do. The body of Christ needs you and your gift!

Chapter 4

Pure From the Blood
of All Men

And indeed, now I know that you all, among whom I have gone preaching the kingdom of God, will see my face no more. Therefore, I testify to you this day that I am innocent of the blood of all men. For I have not shunned to declare to you the whole counsel of God. Therefore take heed to yourselves and to all the flock, among which the Holy Spirit has made you overseers, to shepherd the church of God which He purchased with His own blood (Acts 20:25-28).

In Acts 20:25, Paul told the pastors they would not see him again, which caused them tremendous grief. Verses 36 and 37 say they all wept when they heard this. Their love for Paul as a spiritual father was probably greater than their love for their natural fathers (1 Corinthians

4:15). During the three years Paul was in Ephesus, they were saved and grew up spiritually under his leadership.

As discussed earlier, Paul was the apostle who began the first church at Ephesus, and out of that great church came other churches. These pastors were raised up under Paul's ministry. That is the reason they were sorrowful when Paul announced they would *"see his face no more."*

What they did not realize was they *would* see Paul's face again. After he was delivered out of prison, he would visit them one last time. But at this moment, Paul believed he would never see them again.

PRACTICAL WISDOM

In the previous verses of scripture, it was noted that Paul had avoided the leading of the Holy Spirit in his own life by determining to go to Jerusalem. Nevertheless, what he shared with these pastors in the following verses contains some of the greatest practical wisdom for ministers found in all of the New Testament.

Acts 20:26 says, *"Therefore I testify to you this day that I am innocent...."* Leviticus 17:11 states that *"the life of the flesh is in the blood...."* This means the very life of every human being is found in his or her blood. Therefore, blood represents a person's life. Paul explained he was pure, free from the responsibility of the lives of all men.

How would you like to go to sleep at night knowing you are free from the responsibility of your people? Paul explained how to accomplish this in the next verse, *"For I have not shunned to declare to you the whole counsel of God."*

The word "shunned" is *hupostello*, the same word we found in verse 20 for "kept back." Paul was saying, "I have kept back nothing from you. I have not 'furled the sails' (see Chapter 2) when I came to declare all the counsel of God to you."

When you present everything God has given to you from His Word and hold nothing back, you are then free from the responsibility of your congregation's lives. After you have delivered the Word of God to the people, then the responsibility to live for the Lord is theirs.

Second Corinthians 6:11-13 says, *"O Corinthians! We have spoken openly to you, our heart is wide open. You are not restricted by us, but you are restricted by your own affections. Now in return for the same (I speak as to my children), you also be open."*

Paul was not saying he had an enlarged heart physically, but spiritually. His heart was filled to capacity and overflowing with the Word of God.

Have you ever been so full of God's Word you felt bigger in your spirit than in your body? Smith Wigglesworth, a powerful British evangelist whom God used mightily in the first half of the twentieth century, made the statement, "I am bigger on the inside than I am on the outside." This was Paul's meaning when he said, *"...our heart is wide open."*

When Paul said, *"We have spoken openly to you,"* it is because out of the abundance of the heart the mouth speaks. In other words, "I am not furling the sails with you. Whatever is in my heart, my mouth is speaking to you."

In the next verse Paul continued, *"You are not restricted by us, but you are restricted by your own affections."* A better translation would be, "You are not hindered by us, but you are hindered by your own emotions." What a powerful statement!

The problem with most congregations today is they are emotionally crippled. They are dictated to by their emotions and their lives revolve around how they feel at the moment.

They will praise God if they feel like it. They will study the Bible if they feel like it. They will accept the sermon if they feel like it. Then they will talk about the pastor or anybody else in the congregation if they don't feel like they are doing a good job. They are controlled by their feelings.

The Corinthians were the same way, and Paul exhorted them, "You are not hindered by me. I am not your problem. Your emotions are your problem." In the next verse, he gave them the cure for their problem: *"You also be open."*

In other words, "Stop focusing on how you feel, concentrate on the Word of God, and fill your heart to overflowing with God's Word." You know you are starting to grow in the kingdom of God when you make the decision to live according to God's Word instead of what you feel from moment to moment.

You don't feel like praising God? Speak to yourself, "It doesn't matter how I feel. I'm going to praise and worship the Father in spirit and in truth" (see John 4:23). No longer are you hindered by your emotions; you are letting your heart, which is filled with the Word of God, dictate your actions.

The mark of a mature believer is taking full responsibility for living out the Word of God in his or her life. When a mature believer makes a mistake or fails in some area, their first question is, "God, where did I miss it?"

But the immature believer will flounder, make mistakes and then blame the church or someone else. They blame the pastor for not preaching right. They blame the congregation for not being supportive enough.

That is the reason Paul said to this carnal, immature body of believers in Corinth, "It's not my fault if you are not growing up spiritually. I am not hindering you. Why? Because I poured out to you the Word of God that is within me. Now the responsibility for your lives is in your hands."

THE WHOLE COUNSEL OF GOD

One of the major reasons Paul could boldly declare he was *"pure from the blood of all men"* is found in Acts 20:27. Paul said, *"For I have not shunned to declare to you the whole counsel of God."* The phrase, *"all the counsel of God"* or *"the whole counsel of God,"* means every area of teaching found in the Bible.

Some ministers only focus on one or two of their favorite topics in the Word of God. But Paul instructed the pastors of Ephesus that they had an obligation to teach the whole counsel of God—every area of the Word of God—to fully fulfill their responsibility as a minister to the people.

When a pastor teaches only a few doctrines and ignores the rest of scripture, not only will it produce an imbalanced congregation, but their "blood" will be on his head. For example, if a pastor refuses to preach on sanctification, end times, family, or finances, God will hold that pastor accountable.

As a pastor, you need to deliver the whole Word of God from both the Old and New Testaments, not just the portions you enjoy. Paul commended the pastor at Colosse, Epaphras, who prayed that his congregation *"may stand perfect and complete in all the will of God"* (Colossians 4:12). You can only pray for your people to stand in all the will of God if you are preaching and teaching all the will of God.

Many ministers shy away from preaching certain portions of the Bible because other ministers have taken those areas to an extreme. Pastors may have met believers who were hurt because they followed a ministry that took a certain doctrine and twisted it. Instead of addressing the topic, they avoid it altogether.

Ministers may stay away from controversial doctrines or topics dealing with very private issues in their lives. Or they may simply avoid certain scripture passages in the Word of God because they consider those topics boring.

Jesus compared the Word of God with "our daily bread," or the food we eat every day to maintain our health and receive the energy we need to be productive. Like food in our natural lives, the Bible contains different varieties of spiritual food—from fried chicken to ice cream to spinach!

When we eat natural food, we must eat a balanced diet to be healthy. In school, we learned about the basic food groups and the importance of eating different kinds of foods daily to feel well. We learned a diet consisting only of candy would result in an unhealthy body.

The same principle applies to spiritual food. A congregation will only grow and remain strong by receiving *"all the counsel of God."*

Some may complain when they are served liver and onions, and some may be unwilling to leave the apple pie for the Brussels sprouts! But in the end, there will be a stronger congregation if you explain the importance of a balanced diet of *"all the counsel of God"* (2 Timothy 3:16-17).

The pastor who truly loves his congregation and desires to see every individual excel in every area of their lives will preach and teach everything the Bible has to say. When it comes to the controversial issues or those areas that have been taken to extremes, he will study them out for himself and teach his people the balance from the Word of God.

In dealing with intimate areas, he will tackle these subjects with confidence and boldness, trusting God to give him wisdom in presenting the truth in the most effective way.

And when it is time to teach the areas of God's Word that seem less than exciting, he will pray for his eyes and the eyes of his congregation's understanding to be enlightened to the richness and power in these important doctrines and principles. Usually when a pastor is excited about what he is teaching, it will be contagious, and his congregation will become excited too.

We are living in a day when believers need to know what the Word of God says. Daily, our minds are bombarded through television, movies, publications, and various social media. And the deception, opinions, and philosophies of the world are constantly before us. It is vital to know and understand what God says.

The Holy Spirit challenges us in Hebrews 5:12-14 when He says:

For though by this time you ought to be teach-
ers, you need someone to teach you again the first
principles of the oracles of God; and you have
come to need milk and not solid food. For every-
one who partakes only of milk is unskilled in the
word of righteousness, for he is a babe. But solid
food belongs to those who are of full age, that is,
those who by reason of use have their senses exer-
cised to discern both good and evil.

If you are a pastor or are preparing to step into full-
time ministry, you should be past the battle yourself. You
should have grown in your relationship with God beyond
the milk of the Word to a place where your senses can
"discern both good and evil."

The Bible says in Hebrews 4:12-13 the Word of God
is a *"discerner of the thoughts and intents of the heart. And*
there is no creature hidden from His sight, but all things are
naked and open to the eyes of Him to whom we must give
account." That person is Jesus.

When you are strong in the Word and are walking
with the Lord, very little will escape you. You can discern
deception immediately. If false doctrine is taught, the
Word in you will expose it and eliminate it. God wants
us all to grow to "full age" and to build a solid foundation
from which we can effectively reach this generation with
the gospel. But in order for this to happen, our churches
must be well-fed on a balanced diet, which means *"the*
whole counsel of God."

FEED THE FLOCK

Acts 20:26-28 says: "*Therefore I testify to you this day that I am innocent of the blood of all men.*" Paul continued, "*For I have not shunned to declare to you the whole counsel of God. Therefore, take heed to yourselves and to all the flock, among which the Holy Spirit has made you overseers, to shepherd the church....*"

The Holy Spirit has made you an overseer. The Greek word for "made" is *tithemi,* which means to place or appoint, and the word "overseers" is *episkopos,* which means overseer or bishop. This verse states the Holy Spirit appoints the pastor to oversee the flock. He gives the pastor the vision for that particular local church.

The King James Version of the Bible states verse 28 this way, "*Take heed therefore unto yourselves, and to all the flock, over the which the Holy Ghost hath made you overseers, **to feed the church of God**, which he hath purchased with his own blood.*"

The Greek word for "feed" is *poimen,* which means pastor or shepherd, a clear reference to preaching and teaching the Word of God to the people.

This verse identifies two areas of responsibility for the pastor:

1. Feed: preaching and teaching the Word of God

2. Lead: receiving and carrying out the vision for the church

God called me to pastor, which means a major portion of my time was spent studying God's Word. And I did, to stay before Him in prayer to get direction for the church over which He made me overseer.

It is interesting to note there is no break in the original Greek in Ephesians 4:11 between pastor and teacher. Most scholars agree that "pastor" is a title and "teacher" is the function of the pastor. I stood in the office of a pastor and my job was to teach. Therefore, I was a pastor-teacher. While it is true that you can stand in the office of a teacher without being a pastor (1 Corinthians 12:28), you cannot be a pastor without being a teacher.

Some people think the pastor is primarily a counselor. While it is right for a pastor to do some counseling, that is not his major calling. His primary responsibility is to study God's Word and pray. Then he can lead the people in the will of God and feed them well with His Word.

God raises up congregational members to become deacons, elders, and bishops within the local church body. These men and women are called to assist the pastor by taking on the duties of counseling, visitation, music ministry, and the other functions of the church.

From time to time, the pastor will counsel, visit, and if he is gifted in this way, he may even lead worship. However, his first priority is to the Word of God and prayer. By delegating various ministry opportunities to others, he is able to succeed in study and prayer.

A church member said to me, "You have to get out and visit everyone or the church will fall apart." I responded, "I didn't visit them to get them to come in the first place." People come because they love the Word of God and being in God's presence during church services.

Acts 6:7 says the number of disciples increased, and even many Jewish priests became believers as the Word of God was preached. Why not stick with the plan we know is successful?

This does not exempt pastors from counseling or visiting members of the congregation, but they must prayerfully seek the direction of the Holy Spirit to know when to become involved in these other areas.

Also, if the pastor did everything, no one else could ever be involved in ministry! When you know God has called you to full-time ministry, you do not immediately begin in the pulpit. You start by looking for an area of work in the church. You visit the sick and pray for them, you help lead praise, or become one of the counselors.

From these positions, God will promote you as you are faithful (1 Timothy 3:13). Great missionaries who went out from our church were at one time janitors or operated the sound equipment. There are gifted pastors across the United States who ushered or counseled at the church prior to God calling them out of our local body.

God raises up these people to free the pastor's time for study and prayer. When I would counsel someone, I was only reaching one person. But when I taught the

Word from the pulpit, I was doing my most effective job. I was reaching more people. My anointing was strongest when I was in the pulpit doing the primary thing God called me to do—*feed the flock.*

SUPERNATURAL STRIVING

Romans 15:20 says, *"I have made it my aim to preach the gospel...."* There is a striving to preach the gospel, and to study, pray, and teach the Word of God. The striving is against Satan and the flesh as you try to spend time with God.

Satan opposes the ministry more than anything else. People have told me, "I never had this much opposition when I was running my business. I went into the ministry and it seemed like all hell broke loose!"

The Word of God tells us Satan is the accuser of the brethren. There are many examples in the Bible of him doing this to great spiritual leaders, such as Job (Job 1:9-20) and Joshua, the high priest (Zechariah 3:1-4). He brings the greatest pressure upon spiritual leadership because he knows if he weakens the leader, he can destroy the followers.

Satan also knows your time before God produces a knowledge of the Word coupled with a supernatural ministry. Signs and wonders follow those who spend time waiting on the Lord, and therefore he will try to prevent you from spending that time. You must strive to overcome his hindering tactics and persevere in study and prayer.

Even though there is a cost to a supernatural ministry, the rewards are tremendous. As the power of the Holy Spirit operates through your ministry, unbelievers will accept Jesus Christ, the lame will walk, and the blind will see. This does great damage to Satan's kingdom.

There is also a personal benefit to this striving. Second Peter 1:10 says, *"Therefore, brethren, be even more diligent* [to the Word of God] *to make your call and election sure, for if you do these things you will never stumble."* You will never doubt your salvation or your calling, and your life and ministry will become completely stable and dependable, as you are faithful to the Word and prayer.

Although learning how to enter into God's presence and how to allow His power to work in and through your life varies. You can learn certain principles from others. I know one powerful minister of God who prays in the Spirit many hours each day. His lifestyle encourages the rest of us to pray in the Spirit; but we should not be led by his method, we should be led by the Spirit.

Some ministers fast before services and others eat. Some take a nap, walk alone, or are quiet before the Lord before they minister. They have spent hours developing their relationship with the Lord and striving to understand how the Holy Spirit wants to work through them.

Satan opposes these supernatural ministries because the results are so great. When many people have their needs met, many more will accept Jesus as their Lord and Savior as a result. The devil tries to prevent pastors from spending time studying the Word and communing with the Holy Spirit in prayer.

Often, the moment you sit down to study and pray, every tactic will be used to stop you. You may have instructed your secretary not to disturb you except for an emergency, but you will still have to contend with your flesh.

Satan will see to it that you remember things you need to do around the house, people in the church who should be contacted, and areas of need will loom before your eyes. Things you had not thought about in months will spring up unexpectedly.

If these devices don't succeed in distracting you, your flesh will try to sabotage your efforts. It will try everything from terrible fatigue to the temperature of the room, to keep you from concentrating on Bible study and prayer.

However, your striving and perseverance in study and prayer will produce a close relationship between you and God that builds the solid foundation of an effective, powerful ministry.

WHOSE FLOCK ARE THEY?

We now come to the next point in Acts 20:28: "...*to shepherd the church of God which He purchased with His own blood.*" The ultimate responsibility for the flock is on the

Lord Jesus Christ. He purchased us with His blood, and the entire Church belongs to Him.

He is the Chief Shepherd, the Ultimate Pastor. If the undershepherd makes a mistake, if the pastor fails in some way, Jesus will see to it the church members are ministered to by someone else.

Pastor, you must always remember, the sheep belong to God and He has entrusted them to you. Your job is to lead them and feed them as the Holy Spirit directs, and then it is their responsibility to believe it and live it. I tell my congregation, "If I make a mistake, you still have a Chief Pastor who never fails!"

The pastor did not purchase the Church, God did. Therefore, God is the rightful owner of the Church of Jesus Christ. He purchased the Church with the precious blood of His Son, so that makes all believers very precious to Him. The *"sheep of His pasture,"* the members of the body of Christ, are the most valuable possession God has.

What an awesome privilege it is for God to give a pastor the solemn responsibility to oversee and feed His most precious possession. Some wonder, *But how do you sleep at night?* I could sleep in peace only because I knew that first, they were not my sheep, they were not my people. Second, I am "pure from their blood," because I kept nothing back from them that God had shown me.

Not only did God ask me to prepare the food, He gave me the place to find it! All I could do was pray and present the Word of God, expecting the Holy Spirit to draw them in and meet their needs. I just did my part and trusted God to do His—praying for the sheep to receive it all. That is how I could sleep in peace—*"pure from the blood of all men."*

Throughout the Word, shepherds have never owned the sheep. Moses watched over Jethro's sheep. David watched Jesse's sheep. A pastor is hired by God to watch over His sheep.

Neither does the shepherd supply for the sheep. The owner does. As a pastor, if you are led to begin a building program, you need to go to the Owner for the finances! God supplies for the local church *"according to His riches in glory,"* not according to your riches. The well-being of the sheep belongs to God.

Chapter 5

Take Heed to Yourselves

Paul exhorted the pastors of Ephesus to *"Therefore take heed to yourselves and to all the flock..."* in Acts 20:28. I want to ask you something: In ministry, which comes first, you or your flock?

Carefully examining Acts 20:28, you will discover the Word of God commands you to put yourself before your flock. This doesn't mean you slight your congregation in any way, but you actually aid and assist your people when you take care of yourself and your family first. Obviously, the healthier and more balanced your life is, the more productive and effective your ministry will be.

In Philippians 2:4 Paul continues, *"Let each of you look out not only for his own interests, but also for the interests of others."* A better translation would be, "Don't consider only your own interests, but also consider the interests of others." In other words, we are to set priorities.

In Acts 20:28 and Philippians 2:4, the precedent is established that God wants you to set priorities in your life to take care of yourself. Only then will you be able to take care of the flock to the best of your ability and fulfill your calling with joy.

DAILY SCHEDULES

Ministry is not predictable. There are times I would have loved to work for a fast-food place, where I would just put the meat on the bun and go home. At five o'clock, I would leave the burgers behind and forget about it until the next day.

But in ministry, anything can happen at any moment. Often, adjustments need to be made in both work and private schedules. If you are not diligent to remember you are *"pure from the blood of all men"* (see Chapter 4), you can take the needs home with you. A great mental pressure can arise as you identify with the needs of the people and as you try to figure out how to meet all those needs.

That is why it is vital to have a schedule based on priorities yet flexible enough to take into account the unexpected. The Word of God says, *"Where there is no vision, the people perish"* (Proverbs 29:18 KJV). There needs to be a daily vision to go along with the long-range vision.

Most of the scriptures dealing with time refer to a single day: *"His compassions fail not. They are new every morning..."* (Lamentations 3:22-23). *"...I may daily perform my vows"* (Psalm 61:8). *"Give us this day our daily bread"* (Matthew 6:11). And, *"Exhort one another daily..."* (Hebrews 3:13).

SPIRITUAL WORKAHOLIC

*Yet I considered it necessary to send to you
Epaphroditus, my brother, fellow worker, and
fellow soldier, but your messenger and the one
who ministered to my need; since he was longing
for you all, and was distressed because you had
heard that he was sick. For indeed he was sick
almost unto death; but God had mercy on him,
and not only on him but on me also, lest I should
have sorrow upon sorrow. Therefore I sent him
the more eagerly, that when you see him again
you may rejoice, and I may be less sorrowful.
Receive him therefore in the Lord with all glad-
ness, and hold such men in esteem; because for the
work of Christ he came close to death, not regarding his life, to supply what was lacking in your
service toward me* (Philippians 2:25-30).

In these verses from Philippians 2 there is a rebuke
toward ministers not to become spiritual workahol-
ics. Epaphroditus nearly died because he overworked
himself in the ministry and did not consider his own
well-being.

The phrase *"not regarding his life"* in the Greek literally means he is like a fighter who goes into the ring,
knowing his opponent is much stronger and he is totally
out of shape. He knows he is going to be beaten. This is
exactly what happened to Epaphroditus.

This man was weak, he was tired, and he was sick, but he didn't know when or how to rest. He put the needs of others so high above himself he actually worked himself to the point of death.

Epaphroditus had such a distorted vision of the ministry that he never went to Paul to tell him, "Paul, I'm tired. I'm worn out and sick. I need to take some time off." No, he kept working and would have died if not for Paul's prayer of intercession.

You might be thinking, "I'm glad Epaphroditus rose up in faith and God healed him." But that is not what happened! God healed him because He had mercy on Paul: *"lest he should have sorrow upon sorrow."*

What does *"sorrow upon sorrow"* mean? Paul was already in prison, and he didn't want to lose his friend in addition to what he was already suffering, so God healed Epaphroditus as an act of mercy toward Paul.

In other words, Paul said, "Epaphroditus wasn't healed because he believed God, he was spared on my account. He was acting foolishly and killing himself with work, and I begged for mercy—for him and for me—and God healed him."

A BALANCED LIFE

It is not God's will for you to work yourself into exhaustion for the ministry. I find that across the country ministers are discouraged, ready to give up, and just worn out from tiredness. Some call it "burnout," but this condition does not have to occur. It can be avoided by applying practical wisdom from the Word of God.

I have heard ministers say, "I would rather wear out for God than rust out for the devil." Wait a minute! Why do either one? Why can't you live until ninety, one hundred, or one hundred and ten, and still keep preaching?

People who have a workaholic attitude usually put others under condemnation for not working as hard as they do. Then they either die early, or even worse, they get so burned out and tired they quit the ministry and want nothing to do with it.

Again, Philippians 2:4 says, *"Let each of you look out not only for his own interests, but also for the interests of others."* You can look to yourself *and* to others.

I have noticed many make a choice in ministry. They look only at their own needs or they look only at the needs of others. We should have the mind of Christ. We should consider our own needs as well as the needs of others. There can be a balance.

We are still treasures in earthen vessels. What good will it do you or your congregation if you drop dead at forty-five years old?

I realize many ministers become burned out because they take their eyes off the Lord. But I meet more ministers who have never learned to rest. They will work all day, into the night, every day.

Solomon said, *"To everything there is a season, a time for every purpose under heaven"* (Ecclesiastes 3:1). There is a time to work and there is a time for rest. The man of wisdom will listen to the needs of the flock, the needs of his family, and the needs of his own body. He will know when to take heed to each one.

> *Take heed to yourself and to the doctrine. Continue in them, for in doing this you will save both yourself and those who hear you* (1 Timothy 4:16).

Paul exhorted Timothy to learn to take care of himself. He also exhorted him to continue in the Word, which would save himself and his people. Paul said, "Timothy, if you take good care of yourself, if you live what you preach from the Word of God, not only will you live a balanced, productive, and happy life, you will be doing your congregation a great favor too!"

What is interesting is "yourself" is mentioned before the Word. I consider the Word the highest priority in ministry and have always strongly stressed the importance of it in the believer's life. I shut myself off for hours every day to study and meditate on the Word.

Some ministers don't believe studying the Bible is very important. They will interrupt their study as soon as the phone rings to talk to someone. I take Acts 6:4 literally. We as full-time ministers should *"give ourselves continually* [primarily] *to prayer and to the ministry of the word."*

I would instruct my secretary that during certain hours of the day I could not be disturbed. I would give myself to prayer and study. Then the rest of my working day could be filled with meetings, counseling, or visitation.

Praying and studying the Word of God is one area where I could easily overdose. I could study all day and neglect other things. Then I could go home and study some more, which would deprive my family of the attention they need. A "studyaholic" is as bad as a "workaholic" in the ministry.

Paul wanted Timothy to know it is possible to burn out even with studying the Word! *"Take heed to yourself and to the doctrine* [Word of God]," or "Remember to give yourself some time off, even from the Word of God, Timothy. You need to set aside some time for total relaxation."

No Condemnation in Taking a Vacation!

Many pastors feel guilty about taking a vacation and yet they are happy when members of the church are able to take a vacation. First Peter 5:3 says the pastor is to be an example for the flock. Pastors should not be concerned about what the congregation will think if they take a vacation.

Do you think Paul would ask Timothy and Epaphroditus and the pastors of Ephesus to take heed to themselves and not do it himself? After his first missionary journey, the Bible says Paul took a lengthy sabbatical in Antioch (Acts 14:26-28). Since He had been gone for so long, Paul rested at Antioch. After his second missionary journey to Ephesus, Paul rested again. In fact, Paul came to the pastors' conference in Miletus directly from a vacation!

> *And when he* [Paul] *met us at Assos, we took him on board and came to Mitylene. We sailed from there, and the next day came opposite Chios. The following day we arrived at Samos and stayed at Trogyllium. The next day we came to Miletus* (Acts 20:14-15).

No scripture appears in the Bible by accident. All scripture is given by inspiration of God and is profitable. So, why are these verses included? Paul traveled from one place to another, places we may never have heard of before.

I'll explain why. All of these places were resort areas! Even today they are some of the most beautiful areas in the world, in the warmest regions of the Mediterranean, with the best hotels, finest food, and whitest beaches. And Paul is going on a holiday, traveling from one resort to the next just to rest and relax!

Like our modern resort areas, these islands and cities were filled with sin and with people who needed to meet the Lord. All of these places had great spiritual need.

Take Mitylene, for example. It was the capital city of the island of Lesbos, from which we get the English word "lesbian." It was one of the ancient world's great resort spots for lesbians.

The Bible says that Paul only stopped off the coast of Chios. This was one of the more popular places due to its manufacture of the best wine in the ancient world. Rich people came to relax and dine here, and to enjoy the beautiful climate.

The island of Samos was where the ancient world worshipped Hairoh, a Greek goddess, in the same manner that the Ephesians worshipped Diana. Men would come into the temple with meat offerings and then have sex with the priestesses.

All of the places Paul stopped, though beautiful, had tremendous need for the gospel, but these scriptures do not say, "Paul went to Samos and preached," or "Many were saved at Chios." Why did he go to these places? To lie on the beach and get a tan!

Paul learned to take time off between times of ministry. But so many ministers today cannot lie on the beach without feeling condemned. I can see Paul lying there on the warm sand, covered with suntan lotion, and Luke turning to him and saying, "Paul, look at all these sinners. Don't you think we should witness to them?"

I can just hear Paul respond, "Not today, Luke. It's time to relax, rest, and just enjoy ourselves for a while."

There were times when Paul walked into a group of people and preached, and many were saved. There were also times when he did not witness at all.

I'm not saying Paul never witnessed to anyone during his vacations, but the Word of God does not indicate that he did. Certainly, if the Holy Spirit leads you to minister to someone, no matter where you are or what you are doing, then minister. But if you are on vacation and you are not led to minister, enjoy yourself and relax! Again, as Ecclesiastes 3:1 says, there is a time for everything.

The Bible says there are those in the congregation *"given to hospitality"* (Romans 12:13). Hospitality is part of the Christian life. Hospitality is one of the elements found in Acts chapter 1 that made the early church successful. The early church spent time eating and having fellowship with one another.

Christians ought to have the best fellowship in the world. In fact, their parties ought to put the world's parties to shame! I enjoy just being around other believers and having fun. It is refreshing and brings balance to my life.

I know some Christians who go to a party and try to turn it into a prayer meeting or a Bible study. They feel condemned if they have a good time, as if they are sinning. But Paul relaxed in total peace. He knew God could find someone else to preach while he rested.

Ministers often make the mistake of assuming they are the only one God can use in a particular situation or area. They minister because of the needs they see instead of according to the leading of the Holy Spirit. Not even Jesus was led by the needs of the people. He was led by the Holy Spirit—and He went to parties (John 2:1-2) and took time off (Mark 6:31-32).

I heard one minister say he couldn't bear to leave his congregation. After a few years of preaching every service (he wouldn't even invite guest ministers), he had a physical breakdown. While he was hospitalized, he was under such mental anguish that the church had to be turned over to the associate pastor who had preached very little because the pastor was always in the pulpit.

Later he told me, "That was the best thing that ever happened to me." When I asked him why, he responded, "After being away for a month, I returned to find the church was bigger than when I left. I realized I was not as important as I thought."

Some ministers believe the body of Christ rises and falls on their ministry. But here's a big shock: God got along fine before you came along, and He can get along fine after you are gone! Yes, you are important, unique, and special. And yes, you have your place in the body of Christ. But one of the worst things you can do is to think of yourself more highly than you ought to think (Romans 12:3).

Take a vacation! Take time off! Go to Christian parties once in a while! And trust God that while you are away He can work through the bishops and elders and deacons He has raised up in your church to help you carry out the vision.

I would tell my congregation when I would be taking time off. I take two vacations a year, one in the summer and one in the winter. And then, from time to time, my wife and I would take off for a night or two and spend some time by ourselves. I also attended pastor's conferences or seminars throughout the year.

God not only wants us to have time for spiritual refreshing received at conferences and seminars, He also wants us to have time for natural refreshing, like vacations. Common sense says the more refreshed you are, the more you can give to your people when you return.

FAMILY BEFORE MINISTRY

And whatever you do in word or deed, do all in the name of the Lord Jesus, giving thanks to God the Father through Him. Wives, submit to your own husbands, as is fitting in the Lord. Husbands, love your wives and do not be bitter toward them. Children, obey your parents in all things, for this is well pleasing to the Lord. Fathers, do not provoke your children, lest they become discouraged. Bondservants, obey in all things your masters according to the flesh... (Colossians 3:17-22).

This passage in Colossians 3 sets priorities in our Christian lives: God comes first, then our husband or wife, then our children, and finally our profession. If your profession is full-time ministry, it comes after your relationship with God and your family. If you have a part-time ministry, it comes after your relationship with God, your spouse, your children, and your paying profession.

What a sad thing to win souls for the kingdom of God and lose your wife and/or children. If your family is falling apart, no one would blame you for taking time off from your ministry to work on your family relationships.

This is important: God can get another pastor for your congregation. But you are the *only* husband to your wife and the *only* father your children have.

How many times has the family become jealous of the ministry? If you tell your family you will take a day off and you never do, it causes them to become discouraged. And when you finally do take a vacation, you are so wrapped up in the ministry you can't relax and have a good time or be part of their lives.

In the end, this seemingly dedicated minister pushes himself to a breakdown and drives his family away from himself, the ministry, and the things of God.

When I was a pastor, I used to feel guilty when I was around this type of minister. But that all changed. I took time off away from the church to enjoy my family. I would thank God for them and the staff He provided to run things while I was away. I could do this because I realized that the church I pastored did not rise and fall on me—it sits squarely on the shoulders of Jesus Christ!

JETHRO'S ADVICE

One of the most beautiful examples of a pastor and a congregation is Moses and the nation of Israel. Can you imagine having a church of two to three million people? That is what Moses had. I want you to notice there was only one Moses, one head, even though he pastored a great multitude.

> *And so it was, on the next day, that Moses sat to judge the people; and the people stood before Moses from morning until evening. So when Moses' father-in-law saw all that he did for the people, he said, "What is this thing that you are doing for the people? Why do you alone sit, and all the people stand before you from morning until evening?"* (Exodus 18:13-14)

I think it is interesting Jethro did not dictate to Moses. He said, "I'm going to give you a little advice." Also, he told Moses not only was this not good, but it was going to eventually give him a physical breakdown and then where would the people be?

> *I will give you counsel, and God will be with you: Stand before God for the people, so that you may bring the difficulties to God. And you shall*

teach them the statutes and the laws... (Exodus 18:19-20).

Jethro told Moses that his priorities were all wrong. His greatest ministry was to be an intercessor to God for the people's needs and teach the Word to them. Moses needed to learn what Peter told the multitude in Acts 6:4, *"We will give ourselves continually* [primarily] *to prayer and the ministry of the word."*

Jethro continued:

> *And you shall teach them the statutes and the laws, and show them the way in which they must walk and the work they must do. Moreover you shall select from all the people able men, such as fear God, men of truth, hating covetousness; and place such over them to be rulers of thousands, rulers of hundreds, rulers of fifties, and rulers of tens* (Exodus 18:20-21).

The *"able men,"* who knew the Word of God and feared God, were not to look for a position, but to serve. They were to help Moses have a successful ministry. This is the principle of delegation.

I often receive this question from pastors, "When do I begin to delegate authority?" It is clear, using scripture as our pattern, that you should begin delegating when you have ten people. Give someone else the responsibility to set up and put away the chairs. If you start delegating when you have ten, it will be much easier to delegate when you get to fifty.

If you begin delegating when you have small numbers, by the time you have greater numbers you will know whom you can choose as elders and bishops over major ministries of the church. They will have had the opportunity to prove themselves faithful.

It has been my experience that the longer you wait to delegate, the more difficult it becomes to give up the various responsibilities of the church to others. If you try to build the entire church yourself, when you finally do release responsibilities to others, you will keep such a tight rein on everyone, you will ultimately stifle their creativity and ministry.

It is important to learn to let go and allow God to lead the ones to whom you have given responsibility. Then the confidence you place in them as ministers will encourage them to do the best job they can.

When you let go at ten, there is not as much at stake. It doesn't matter if the chairs are not as straight as you would have placed them. You can ask the helper to straighten them. But do not do it yourself! If you learn the principle of delegation at ten with setting up chairs, it will be much easier to turn over the counseling to others as the membership increases.

Exodus 18:22 continues Jethro's talk with Moses:

*And let them judge the people at all times. Then
it will be that every great matter they shall bring
to you, but every small matter they themselves
shall judge. So it will be easier for you, for they
will bear the burden with you.*

God has not called you to minister to everyone. He
has called you to make sure everyone is ministered to.
The staff of the church, whether paid or volunteer, should
be able to eliminate 90 to 95 percent of the problems,
and the pastor can easily handle the other 5 percent. This
allows the pastor to spend the time he needs in the Word
and prayer.

Concluding, Jethro says in Exodus 18:23:

*If you do this thing, and God so commands you,
then you will be able to endure, and all this people
will also go to their place in peace.*

Pastor, if you delegate, you and your congregation are
going to live long, peaceful lives!

If you are burning out your volunteers, something is
wrong. Try to rotate volunteers so they have time with
their families and can be fresh to enjoy their ministry.

We would ask our volunteers to commit to work for
a designated length of time. For example, those volun-
teering to work with children agree to participate for one
year. When one year has passed, they have an option of
leaving or committing for another year. In this way, both

the volunteer and the paid staff know the extent of the volunteer's obligation in the department.

In some cases, I know of volunteers who became discouraged and left the church. Leadership of the church took advantage of their willingness to serve. This is something every pastor should try to avoid.

On the other hand, if you are a volunteer minister in the church, you should *"Take heed unto yourself."* Use common sense and set priorities to live a balanced life. Then your volunteer work will not become a burden to you or your family.

I used to monitor myself by asking myself:

- Am I the same today as I was when I took the church?
- Do I spend as much time in the Word and prayer now as I did then?
- Are my priorities in line?
- Am I living a balanced life?
- Do I spend as much time with my family as I did then?
- Am I delegating what needs to be delegated?
- Am I breaking away for times of spiritual refreshing and taking vacations for times of physical refreshing?

These principles are laid out in the Word of God so we can live a long time and be as productive as possible. After all, Moses' eye was not dim at one hundred and twenty years old, and Joshua conquered a mountain at the age of eighty-five.

Chapter 6

WATCH AND REMEMBER

For I know this, that after my departure savage wolves will come in among you, not sparing the flock. Also from among yourselves men will rise up, speaking perverse things, to draw away the disciples after themselves. Therefore watch, and remember that for three years I did not cease to warn everyone night and day with tears (Acts 20:29-31).

Paul begins this scripture passage from Acts 20:29 with a confident declaration, *"For I know this...."* The Holy Spirit had revealed to Paul that after his departing *"...savage wolves will come in among you, not sparing the flock."*

Paul was warning the pastors of Ephesus that *"savage wolves"* were about to enter the church. The word "savage" means vicious and cruel. They *"come in,"* which means they are going to come from outside the church.

Wolves are unbelievers that *"come in"* to the local church from the outside. Later, in verse 30, Paul will discuss other false teachers and prophets who will rise up from inside the church. These false teachers and prophets are believers who Satan is able to use because of their pride, in an attempt to destroy the church from the inside.

In Acts 20:31, Paul commanded the pastors to watch for possible trouble. Remember, externally or internally, the enemy is always working to try to break the power of what God is doing in the local church by causing confusion and disunity among the staff and the congregation.

WOLVES

The *"savage wolves will come in among you"* are unbelievers. Satan sends them into a church for the specific purpose of dividing and destroying that local body of believers. Jesus called them wolves in sheep's clothing (Matthew 7:15).

Jesus said they come dressed in sheep's clothing—not shepherd's clothing. They try to infiltrate the congregation, acting and sounding like one of the sheep, but secretly seeking to lead the sheep away from God's appointed shepherd and the faith.

Those most influenced are usually the spiritual babies who are not knowledgeable about the basic doctrines of the Word of God. Wolves do not eat shepherds; they eat sheep. They come in to capture the hearts and minds of the unsuspecting and undiscerning church members to draw them away, causing division and church splits.

Of course, the wolf behind all wolves is Satan, the one who *"comes in among you, not sparing the flock."* His representatives, discussed in verse 29, are unbelievers who come into the church looking and talking like Christians.

These wolves will show up in church acting and talking just like the rest of the sheep, being very religious as they talk about love and unity. Slowly but surely, they inject their false teaching and wrong attitude into the minds of those they befriend, causing strife and division in the congregation.

DECEIVED AND DECEIVING OTHERS

In Acts 20:30, Paul says, *"Also from among yourselves,"* or those in ministry, *"will rise up, speaking...."* The words "rise up" speak of pride. Another more vicious tactic the devil uses to try to destroy the local church is through a believer who is puffed up in pride.

In my opinion, one of the greatest tragedies in the church is when a person just beginning in ministry has a great victory, sees a great move of God in their lives, and then tries to get ahead of God by promoting themselves.

I have often observed a person who has had a tremendous spiritual experience or success in ministry, and then they decide they are ready to pastor a church. In essence, they call themselves into the ministry, establish a church somewhere, and then experience a great failure.

One victory does not make a ministry! Every believer can have signs and wonders follow them if they believe and act on God's Word (Mark 16:17). But being called into full-time ministry is a sovereign act of God. It bears repeating again and again—if God does not promote you, you are not promoted.

If you call yourself into the ministry, you must keep yourself in the ministry. It is challenging enough to be in ministry with God supporting you. Without Him, it is nearly impossible. There is absolutely no fulfillment in it!

The Bible says, *"Therefore humble yourselves under the mighty hand of God, that He may exalt you in due time"* (1 Peter 5:6). In other words, when you are faced with a choice to take the high road of exalting yourself, or the low road of humbling yourself, choose the low road. Let the Lord promote you.

You ask, "What should I do while I wait?" Study the Word of God. Get involved helping in your church. Let the Lord open the doors for you.

A powerful passage of scripture is found in 1 Samuel 15:17. Samuel had come to confront Saul, who had disobeyed the Lord's command by not killing Agag, the evil king. Samuel's heart was broken over Saul's disregard for the Lord's command. He said, *"When you were little in your own eyes, were you not head of the tribes of Israel? And did not the Lord anoint you king over Israel?"*

Think of yourself as *"little in your own sight."* That is one of the most important things you can do as a minister. You say, "But the Bible says I'm the righteousness of God in Him" (2 Corinthians 5:21). That's right! In God's sight you are! It is great to know this is how the Father sees you. But in your own sight, you are to see yourself as small.

Understand something, God did not humble Jesus. Philippians 2:7-9 says Jesus *"made Himself of no reputation, taking the form of a bondservant, and coming in the likeness of men. And being found in appearance as a man, **He humbled Himself** and became obedient to the point of death, even the death of the cross. Therefore God also has highly exalted Him and given Him the name which is above every name."*

Do you want God to exalt you? Humble yourself. Not only is taking the low road easier in the long run, but you will also defeat any temptation to become like the believer who "rises up" with pride. Those who walk in pride become deceived and can be used by Satan to deceive others in the congregation.

Second Timothy 3:13-14 says, *"But evil men and impostors will grow worse and worse, deceiving and being deceived. But you must continue in the things which you have learned and been assured of, knowing from whom you have learned them."*

Essentially, Paul told Timothy, "If you want to keep from being deceived, continue to study the Word of God and follow after those who are faithfully teaching you God's Word." Without knowledge of the Word of God, a believer can easily be deceived.

Being deceived means believing a lie to be the truth. The lie can be a false doctrine, a false prophecy, a supernatural experience originating from demons not the Holy Spirit, or a thought or idea that does not come from God.

When a false teacher or prophet rises up within a church, it is more grievous than when a wolf enters in from the outside because those who are doing the damage are children of God. Although they are born again and have been filled with God's Spirit, they willingly choose to believe what they want to believe instead of heeding warnings from the Holy Spirit and living humbly according to the Word of God.

It is sad, but many of these people genuinely believe what they are doing is right and they are on a divine mission to free the body of Christ from some misconception or bondage.

They don't realize Satan's purpose is to use them to distract other believers with false doctrine, *"deceiving spirits and doctrines of demons"* (1 Timothy 4:1). In some cases, they pull congregational members away from the faith and the local church while building their own ministry empire.

One important point I need to mention is there are many solid ministries of integrity who have meetings outside the local church, but their purpose is to add to what the local church is already accomplishing in a church member's life.

They are not seeking to draw people away from the local church. Instead, they encourage believers to get involved in a lócal body of believers and to use the knowledge of the Word of God that is being taught at their meetings in their own churches.

THERE'S NOTHING NEW UNDER THE SON

"Also from among yourselves men will rise up, speaking per-verse things..." (Acts 20:30). Many people today preach and teach what they refer to as "revelation knowledge" but they are really *"speaking perverse things."* In essence, they are taking the Word of God and twisting it to teach their own so-called "new and exciting revelation." They are really using God's Word to exalt themselves.

One tactic of the devil is to pressure ministers into finding something new, exciting, or funny for their people to hear. This leads them to manufacture their own revelations. Or they may take another's sound teaching, and in trying to create something sensational from it, they are *"speaking perverse things."*

The number of doctrines found in the Word of God is limited, but it will take eternity for us to know the depth and breadth of each one.

Ephesians 2:7 says, *"That in the ages to come He might show the exceeding riches of His grace in His kindness toward us through Christ Jesus."* When I hear a minister say he has received a new revelation from the Word of God that no one else has ever received, I wonder if his motive is to promote himself rather than the message.

Another trap ministers fall into is trying to preach something new and exciting *"...to draw away the disciples after themselves"* (Acts 20:30). In other words, to draw crowds. Some people believe a minister who draws great numbers of people must be legitimate. But numbers do not make a ministry. Truth makes a ministry. Integrity in word and deed make a ministry.

I would rather have five people following me as I preach the truth than five thousand people following the preaching of *"perverse things."* Notice, again verse 30, *"...to draw the away disciples after themselves."* These ministers are looking for disciples to follow them—not Jesus.

This verse describes those who distort the Word to make it sensational, hoping to draw disciples away from the church and to themselves. They are building their own kingdom, not God's.

Another indication that a minister's priorities and motives are wrong is if their objective is to begin a church by drawing away members from another congregation.

DESPISING GOVERNMENT

In 2 Peter 2:9, Peter addressed the same problem. *"Then the Lord knows how to deliver the godly out of temptations and to reserve the unjust under punishment for the day of judgment."* The "unjust" refers to the wolf who comes in from outside the church—the unbeliever who acts like a believer in order to divide and destroy the church.

Peter continued, "*And especially those who walk according to the flesh in the lust of uncleanness and despise authority. They are presumptuous, self-willed. They are not afraid to speak evil of dignitaries*" (verse 10). This verse describes the believer who rises up in pride within the church.

"*And especially,*" means it is far worse to deal with a false teacher or prophet (believer) than a wolf (unbeliever), and more grievous to be persecuted by a Christian than an unbeliever. In ministry, your worst enemies will be other believers who are out of fellowship with God. Why? Because they are the most miserable people on earth!

An unbeliever can sin, rebel against God, and not feel convicted because sinning is their nature. But the Holy Spirit of God and a new, regenerated spirit abide within the believer. There is a continual conflict between the carnal, fleshly nature and the Spirit of God in them.

The carnal believer is trying to get satisfaction from giving in to the flesh, but satisfaction will only be found in returning to fellowship with the Lord and walking day by day with God. Being out of fellowship with the Lord brings constant frustration and misery.

Carnal Christians may pretend everything is fine, but they are deceiving themselves and they know it on the inside. They walk "*according to the flesh in the lust of uncleanness"*—not restraining physical appetites, whether for sex, money, fame, food, drink, etc.—*"and despise authority."*

We now come to the root of the problem: carnal believers cannot take instruction or submit to authority— they *"despise authority,"* or *"government"* as the King James Version states. The reason they are out of fellowship with God is because they refuse to submit themselves to those whom God has placed in authority over them. By resisting and rebelling against authority, they are resisting and rebelling against God, who established those authorities.

Because carnal believers are not in intimate relationship with the Father and avoid having their sin confronted by the Word of God, they are totally insecure. Jesus said they have *"no root in themselves"* (see the parable of the sower, Matthew 13:18-23). There is no foundation of the Word in their lives. They have nothing to stand on.

Consequently, when it comes to either choosing the Word of God or their own ideas and fleshly desires, believers who have no true security in God will go with their carnal thinking and ways. This puts them in a position to be deceived and to deceive others—to *"rise up, speaking perverse things"* (Acts 20:30).

However, a Christian who is secure in God, who studies to show himself approved (2 Timothy 2:15) and knows who he is in Christ, is secure with other people and has no problem submitting to authority because he is confident in who he is as a believer.

There are also those immature believers who may not know the Word of God well enough to understand their attitudes are self-centered and self-seeking. These misguided and misled sheep may really believe they are following the Lord, when in reality they are following their own thoughts or feelings rather than submitting to those in authority.

The Word of God says we are to obey all those in authority over us unless we are asked to do something that clearly violates the Word of God (see Chapter 11). Through the principle of delegation, the Holy Spirit will work through a chain of command (see Chapter 5).

When you go against an elder, you go against the pastor who gave him his authority. When you rebel against the pastor, you rebel against Jesus Christ, who gave the pastor his authority—and against God the Father, the Source of all authority!

Does rebelling against God the Father's authority sound familiar? This is exactly what Lucifer did! And when Lucifer rebelled, declaring he would exalt his throne above God's (Isaiah 14:13-14), he became Satan, God's adversary. When you rebel against God-given authority, you are acting in league with His adversary, the devil. In 1 Timothy 3:6 we are told that the root of all rebellion is pride.

Second Peter 2:10 continues, *"They are presumptuous, self-willed. They are not afraid to speak evil of dignitaries."* This is what happens when believers go against the Word of God to satisfy their own selfish desires. They become *"presumptuous,"* thinking they know more than the pastor; *"self-willed,"* believing their way is better than the pastor's; and they are *"not afraid to speak evil of dignities,"* they gossip and malign the pastor and others who are God's anointed and appointed leaders.

These believers are in open rebellion against the pastor and the Word that is taught. You ask, "But what if a minister or pastor is out of line or teaching error?" Pray about it and speak to him privately with an attitude of submission. Don't speak about it in rebellion or talk about it with others! After speaking to him privately, leave the issue in God's hands. He will either change the situation, change you, or move you to another church.

The closer you get to ministers and their ministries, you discover they all have problems and weak areas because we are all human! But I have learned we are not to speak against them. They are God's anointed. He is working in them and through them just like He is working in and through you. Pray for them, reminding yourself you too have weak areas.

The accuser of the brethren is Satan. When you accuse the other believers, you are falling in league with him. Like Satan, these rebellious ones who do not understand or respect authority, who have been deceived and are deceiving others, are always looking for a way to be exalted to a higher position. They try to manufacture their own calling, ministry, and position in leadership, but

Satan's hidden agenda is to use them to divide and disrupt the church they attend.

THE ROD AND THE STAFF

At this point you may be asking, "How do I handle these types of situations? What do I do when I see a wolf in my congregation? And how do I keep balanced so I am not seeing a wolf—a false teacher or false prophet—in every troubling situation that arises? Is there some way of preventing all of this?"

In Acts 20:31 Paul says, *"Therefore **watch, and remember** that for three years I did not cease to warn everyone night and day with tears."* A pastor, like a faithful shepherd, is to watch over the sheep diligently, remembering the Bible warns of possible attacks from within and without the church.

A pastor should not be suspicious of everyone, but he is also not to be oblivious to signs that a deceiver—a wolf—is at work among his people. Like a faithful shepherd, he should remain alert for strange doctrines, ideas, or practices that are circulating in the congregation, and be aware of the ministries that pass through town.

The shepherd, mentioned repeatedly in the Bible, carried both a rod and a staff while caring for his flock. The staff was for the sheep. It had a crook in it so when a sheep was caught in the rocks or bushes, the shepherd simply hooked it around its neck and lifted it out of danger. The rod was for the wolves. It was a club used to beat the wolves until they fled from the flock.

The Word of God is the pastor's staff. In 2 Timothy 3:16-17 we are told, *"All Scripture is given by inspiration of God, and is profitable for doctrine, for reproof, for correction, for instruction in righteousness, that the man of God may be complete* [mature], *thoroughly equipped for every good work."*

Whether one member has gone astray and a counselor or the pastor speaks the Word of God to them privately, or many members have been influenced and the pastor is led to teach on the subject that is being distorted, speaking God's Word is the most effective destroyer of *"deceiving spirits and doctrines of demons"* (1 Timothy 4:1).

The Bible repeatedly emphasizes the importance of knowing God's Word because God's people are destroyed for a lack of knowledge (Hosea 4:6). By preaching and teaching the Word of God week after week, by *"holding nothing back"* and giving his congregation *"the whole counsel of God,"* a pastor is expressing the greatest compassion and concern for his congregation.

One of the most crucial prayers a pastor prays for his congregation is after his sermon, not before. In Colossians 4:12, Paul commends Epaphras, the pastor of the church at Colosse, who is *"always laboring fervently for you in prayers, that you may stand perfect and complete in all the will of God."*

Most pastors pray before the service. They pray for their messages to be powerful and anointed, for the Holy

Spirit to move during the services in a mighty way. But Epaphras also prayed after the people heard the Word of God. He prayed they would become mature and successful by living what they had heard.

Knowledge of the Word of God builds a hedge of protection around a believer's life and causes discernment of good and evil (Hebrews 5:14). Then when a believer goes astray, the pastor gently places God's Word around his neck to bring him back into the fold.

The rod is the exercise of the pastor's authority over those who want to divide and destroy his congregation. Paul told Titus, *"For there are many insubordinate, both idle talkers and deceivers, especially those of the circumcision, whose mouths must be stopped, who subvert* [overturn] *whole households* [churches]*, teaching things which they ought not, for the sake of dishonest* [money] *gain* (Titus 1:10-11). Verse 13 continues, *"... Therefore rebuke them sharply...."*

There have been times when I had to use my pastoral authority to stop false prophets from prophesying because they were disrupting the flow of the Holy Spirit during the service. Occasionally, I have had to instruct the ushers to remove them from the auditorium.

There have been other times when I would allow a member of the congregation to attend the services but would not allow the person to participate in a ministry capacity in any area of the church because the person had used their ministry position to extort money from members of the congregation.

I also had the painful duty of firing members of my staff who became entangled in sin or strange doctrines because many members of the church were being hurt by their ministry.

David said of the Chief Shepherd, "...*Your rod and Your staff, they comfort me*" (Psalm 23:4). The sheep are comforted knowing the shepherd carries both the rod and the staff. A congregation develops a confidence and security knowing not only is their pastor faithful to pray over them and give them the Word of God, he also will not hesitate to stop a wolf—a false teacher or false prophet trying to infiltrate the church.

There is great comfort for God's people when their pastor will "*watch and remember*" (Acts 20:31).

Chapter 7

Paul's Final Words and Departure

So now, brethren, I commend you to God and to the word of His grace, which is able to build you up and give you an inheritance among all those who are sanctified. I have coveted no one's silver or gold or apparel. Yes, you yourselves know that these hands have provided for my necessities, and for those who were with me. I have shown you in every way, by laboring like this, that you must support the weak. And remember the words of the Lord Jesus, that He said, "It is more blessed to give than to receive" (Acts 20:32-35).

Paul began this portion of his message by saying, *"So now, brethren, I commend you to God...."* The word "commend" actually means to make a deposit, to entrust. He says, "Men, you have been entrusted to me for the last few years, but now I'm getting ready to leave. So, I deposit you with God, and not only with God, but also with the word of His grace."

As a pastor, you have the right to deposit your people *"with God and the word of His grace"* just as Paul did with these pastors. After you have opened the Word of God and taught them everything God has given you, you can place them squarely in the care of the Word you have given them.

However, it is very important to realize you can only deposit people into what you teach. Into the Word you give them. In other words, if you don't teach them about the new birth, then you cannot believe God for their salvation. If you don't teach the doctrine of righteousness, you cannot expect them to live according to it.

Since Paul preached grace, he could deposit them into *"the word of His grace."* And because he taught them about trusting the Lord, he could deposit them into the hands of the Lord.

This is a great principle to remember, especially for evangelists. It is often impossible to stay with somebody and help them grow spiritually after they are saved and delivered. You can recommend a good church to them and turn them over to pastors, but a demon can still whisper the lie that they will never make it.

Satan will taunt you with accusations, "Sure, you may bring them into the kingdom but then you desert them. You are leaving them with no knowledge of the Word! Maybe they *were* healed, but they will lose their healing by the end of the week. So what if their craving for drugs is gone. Just give them a few days and they will be back on the streets again!"

That is when you declare, according to God's Word, you are depositing them into the hands of God and to the Word of His grace. You remind the devil the Holy Spirit will lead other believers to encourage them. You have done your part, and now you can have peace that God will take care of the rest. If He is faithful enough to bring you across their path, He will be faithful to bring whoever else He chooses to speak a word in season or to pray with them if they become discouraged.

Paul was faced with a similar situation because he could not permanently remain in Ephesus to encourage and counsel these pastors. Therefore, he deposited them *"to God, and into the word of His grace, which is able to build you up...."*

Paul knew that in placing the pastors into God's care, he was entrusting them into far better hands than his own. *"The word of His grace,"* which he had poured into these ministers, would be present to edify and build them up long after Paul had departed. Where Paul could have occasionally disappointed and failed them because of his humanness, the Word of God and His grace would *never* fail them.

In the same way Paul commended the pastors at Ephesus into God's care, these same pastors would need to deposit their congregations into the Word they would preach. The grace of God that would keep these pastors would also keep their people as they were confronted with difficult times. The grace of God would carry them farther than any one minister could!

FINANCIAL INTEGRITY

In Acts 20:32, Paul indicates there is a special reward for pastors—*"an inheritance among all those who are sanctified"* (further study in Chapter 10). He continued in verse 33 saying, *"I have coveted no one's silver or gold or apparel."*

Why would Paul make such a statement? It was because he had been given silver, gold, and apparel! On numerous occasions, he had received many costly and precious gifts of love and appreciation as he ministered to people.

God's Word, ministered through your life, can so bless people that they will want to give you something valuable to show how grateful they are to God for your ministry. This aspect of ministry is a tremendous blessing, but it also bears a great responsibility. The minister must guard his heart to keep from coveting these things.

When Paul said, *"I have coveted no man's silver or gold or apparel,"* he was setting a standard for financial integrity in ministry. Money is one of the most important and sensitive areas in a church. Paul choosing to discuss finances in the ministry just before his departure was no accident.

One of Satan's favorite ways to destroy a church is through financial mismanagement. He particularly likes to lead a pastor or minister astray, either through ignorance or through covetousness, and then glowingly expose it to the entire world.

Today, with the vast media coverage of every scandal that occurs in the Church, it is vital that *every* church and *every* minister keep their financial affairs legally and morally in order.

One way we accomplished this in the church I pastored is to have an annual audit by a reputable financial firm in town. We would distribute the annual report at the church's yearly business meeting. This allowed us to give an account to staff, congregational members, the public, or government agencies requesting current financial information.

A yearly audit is somewhat costly, but it is well worth the peace of mind it affords the pastor and his congregation. If you pastor a small church and cannot afford an audit, I would urge you to keep your books straight and be open about them with your congregation. Or perhaps someone in your congregation would volunteer their time for this task. What is most important is to make sure the finances of the church are legally in order and readily available.

It is also important that you, as the pastor, set the standard for moral integrity in finances. The focus of your ministry should always be to minister to the people, *not* to get the people to minister to you in their finances.

A pastor must teach his congregation what the Word of God has to say about prosperity and giving as part of the whole counsel of God. This involves teaching the people how to live in God's system of prosperity. It is essential for their success in the Christian life.

However, if a minister begins to major on finances whenever he teaches and is constantly making pleas for money, his priorities are out of balance. If your motive is to minister to the people to meet their needs, their desire will be to give something in return.

Whenever there was a financial need in the church, I reminded myself the people were not my sheep. I was hired by their Owner to watch over and feed this portion of His people, but the ultimate responsibility was His.

Therefore, I would go to Him and say, "Lord, You have a problem here. I have been faithful to feed *Your sheep* Your Word, and You told me in Your Owner's Manual You would supply all my needs according to Your riches in glory by Christ Jesus. So, speak to Your people about what they should do. They know Your voice, and they respect Yours much more than they do mine."

In this way, you don't have to keep pressing the congregation to give money all the of the time. Teach them about giving, pray for them, and then the responsibility is not on you—it is between the people and God. Remember, God has called you and He will promote and prosper you, not your congregation.

Paul continues by telling the pastors, "*...you yourselves know, that these hands have provided for my necessities...*" (Acts 20:34). Paul reminded the pastors there were times when the ministry did not support him financially, and he had to find a secular job.

While in Corinth, Paul made tents to support himself while he preached to the wealthy Corinthian believers. Paul stressed a very important point to these pastors. Some of the ministers probably didn't want to get a job or were too proud to work because they wanted to instantly be in full-time ministry.

Pastors often ask me, "When should I go into full-time ministry and give up my secular job?" I always tell them, "When the church is able to support you financially. When it can pay all of your bills."

Many ministers feel it is below their dignity to go out and get a job, but Paul is saying that he not only supported himself, he also supported his entire ministry team: "*Yes, you yourselves know that these hands have provided for my necessities, and for those who were with me.*"

When starting a new work, it not only may be a financial necessity to have an outside job, but also a reassurance to the people. You are demonstrating, in a tangible way, money is not your motive in beginning a church and that you are just as committed to the church as any of the members.

When enough finances come into the church to support the pastor, he can and should make his income from the preaching of the Word of God. At this point, the pastor's ministry of the Word of God should become just as demanding as any other job he may have had (see Chapter 9). He should put maximum effort into studying the scriptures and fulfilling the vision of the church (1 Thessalonians 2:9-12).

THE HEART OF A PASTOR

In Acts 20:35, Paul quoted Jesus as he shared with the pastors. *"I have shown you in every way, by laboring like this, that you must support the weak. And remember the words of the Lord Jesus, that He said, 'It is more blessed to give than to receive.'"*

This statement was handed down to Paul from one of the apostles of Jesus. Paul was fully satisfied that this was what Jesus said.

It is important to note that just before stepping on board the ship to sail away, Paul was led of the Holy Spirit to share this particular quote from Jesus. Paul's very last words to them involved keeping their hearts pure in the area of finances.

A minister's heart is kept pure when his focus is on meeting the needs of the people. But a minister's heart is defiled when he begins devising ways to get money out of the people and when he takes advantage of the poor and weak to meet the budget of his church or ministry.

In essence, Paul was saying, "If you begin looking for what the people can give to you, instead of what you can give to the people, your heart motive is wrong. Jesus said, *"It is more blessed to give than to receive."*

Unfortunately, there are some ministers today using the gospel for personal gain. Others have ministries that have grown so large they have resorted to fundraising tactics to enable them to finance the machinery of their ministries.

These ministers take verses of scripture, many times out of context or to an extreme, and use them to motivate believers into giving into their ministry. They have forgotten their hearts should be toward giving to the people, rather than receiving from them.

When a pastor recognizes some of his congregational members are being taken in by unscriptural teachings, he must defend his sheep with the staff, the Word of God (see Chapter 6). Teach the Word. Let the people see for themselves how God's financial system works—*when* to give and not to give, and *how* to give.

If it is necessary to expose the error in certain ministries, teach the Word on that subject and let the Bible be the judge of their financial practices.

With highly publicized accounts of the financial misdeeds in ministry today, an important passage of scripture to remember is found in 1 Kings 19. Elijah had become discouraged and complained to God that he was the only one in Israel who was serving the Lord. When ministers fall, often it becomes such a media event that it seems as though all ministers are corrupt and very few have hearts for God and serving the people.

But God corrected Elijah, informing him there were still over seven thousand more in Israel who were serving the Lord (1 Kings 19:18). I am convinced, for every minister who falls, there are multiplied many more serving God with all their heart, soul, mind, and strength.

When sensationalized media reports try to discourage believers, it is important for pastors to remind their congregations of Elijah. Remind them no matter what Elijah had seen, heard, or thought, God's Word prevailed— seven thousand had not bowed their knee.

The heart of the pastor should be a mirror reflection of the heart of Jesus, who loved us so much He gave His life to save us. One of the ways I have come to recognize those who are called to pastor is by the tremendous love for people that pours out from deep in their hearts. They are constantly giving to others, and their chief desire is to see people's needs met.

This is one of the reasons pastoring is such a rewarding and fulfilling calling. Pastors are extremely blessed because *"it is more blessed to give than to receive";* and as said before, when the needs of the people are being met, they joyfully want to give into the ministry in return.

AN EMOTIONAL FAREWELL

The account of Paul's farewell and departure for Jerusalem is found in Acts 20:36-38. He and these elders believe that they will not see each other after this, and it is a very emotional time for all of them.

And when he had said these things, he knelt down and prayed with them all. Then they all wept freely, and fell on Paul's neck and kissed him, sorrowing most of all for the words which he spoke, that they would see his face no more. And they accompanied him to the ship (Acts 20:36-38).

I want you to notice how emotional these ministers were, and how demonstrative they were about their feelings for Paul. These verses clearly show ministers can and should express emotions.

Over and over again I teach that pastors are human, that they have a gift to teach the Word, but they must live it like every believer. Well, pastors have emotions too! Even though we live according to the Word of God and not according to our emotions, we can nevertheless express them when it is appropriate.

Some pastors believe they must always be strong for their congregations. And they will appear successful before other ministers if they maintain a certain distance. But it is ironic that the strongest and boldest are not afraid to show their emotions or to be affectionate with their people and with other ministers because they know who they are in Christ.

I believe the Holy Spirit included these verses to encourage tenderness and affection among ministers. Paul and the pastors of Ephesus were open and honest with one another in every way. As the pastors of Ephesus wept, hugged Paul, and kissed him good-bye, they had no problem expressing their sorrow about his leaving or their love for him. Neither were they concerned about their personal reputations because of having expressed their feelings. After all, pastors should walk in the liberty of the Holy Spirit more than anybody!

Chapter 8

THE SHEPHERD AND
HIS SHEEP

*The elders who are among you I exhort, I who
am a fellow elder and a witness of the sufferings
of Christ, and also a partaker of the glory that
will be revealed: Shepherd the flock of God which
is among you...* (1 Peter 5:1-2).

We have been studying about what Paul had to say to the
pastors at Ephesus in Acts 20:17-38. Peter also addressed
pastors in 1 Peter 1:1, *"Peter, an apostle of Jesus Christ, to the
pilgrims of the Dispersion in Pontus, Galatia, Cappadocia,
Asia, and Bithynia."*

The *"pilgrims"* are born-again Jews who were living in
these Gentile countries. They were Jewish merchants and
businessmen who had left Israel in order to make a better
living, and they received Jesus as their Messiah through
Christian missionaries. Peter is writing to encourage
them in their newfound faith.

The words of Peter to the pastors of these scattered Jews (1 Peter 5:1-6) are closely linked with the words of Paul to the pastors of Ephesus (Acts 20:17-38). Although Paul is speaking primarily to Gentile pastors and Peter is speaking primarily to Jewish pastors, they both cover the same basic areas.

Peter addressed, *"The elders who are among you"* (1 Peter 5:1), just as Paul *"sent to Ephesus and called the elders of the church"* (Acts 20:17).

Peter continued, *"I who am a fellow elder."* The Greek word for "elder" is *sumpresbuteros*, which means fellow elder. Even though he is an apostle, like Paul, Peter identifies himself as a fellow minister and a fellow pastor.

In Acts 20:32, Paul referred to the pastors from Ephesus as his *"brethren."* Neither Peter nor Paul set themselves above the rest of the pastors, although it is obvious, they were exhorting and encouraging the pastors as spiritual fathers. When Peter mentioned he was *"a witness of the sufferings of Christ,"* he was acting as a spiritual father. Peter shared his personal testimony of watching as Jesus was beaten and crucified. Peter also revealed he was on the Mount of Transfiguration, making the statement, *"...and also a partaker of the glory that shall be revealed"* (1 Peter 5:1).

Peter, James, and John had personally witnessed the supernatural appearance of Elijah and Moses. Peter watched as Jesus was transfigured into all of His glory (Matthew 17:1-3).

After sharing this testimony, Peter emphasized to the pastors to *"Shepherd the flock of God* which is among you...."* This is the same exhortation Paul gave the pastors of Ephesus in Acts 20:28. Both Paul and Peter stressed the most important responsibility of the pastor is to feed the sheep—to preach and teach the Word of God to the congregation.

Another important point made in this verse is a pastor has only one flock. Peter said, *"Feed the flock of God which is among you...."* It is unscriptural to have two flocks, three flocks, or to be the pastor over more than one church on a permanent basis.

There is absolutely nothing wrong with a pastor of one church starting another church. A missionary may oversee several churches for a period of time. But in these cases, a pastor should be found for the other church or churches as soon as possible, because God has called one pastor to one body of believers. An apostle, like Paul, may oversee a group of churches he founded, but each church should have its own pastor.

Three different types of the pastor and the local church are found in the Word of God: 1) Jesus and the universal Church; 2) the head and the body; and 3) the husband and the wife. Is Jesus the Chief Shepherd over more than one flock? Is a head attached to more than one body? Is a husband married to more than one wife? No! Neither should a pastor oversee more than one congregation.

PETER REMEMBERS

So when they had eaten breakfast, Jesus said to Simon Peter, "Simon, son of Jonah, do you love Me more than these?"

He said to Him, "Yes, Lord; You know that I love You."

He said to Him, "Feed My lambs."

He said to him again a second time, "Simon, son of Jonah, do you love Me?"

He said to Him, "Yes, Lord; You know that I love You."

He said to him, "Tend My sheep."

He said to him the third time, "Simon, son of Jonah, do you love Me?" Peter was

grieved because He said to him the third time, "Do you love Me?"

And he said to Him, "Lord, You know all things; You know that I love You."

Jesus said to him, "Feed My sheep" (John 21:15-17).

Peter had adopted the phrase, *"Feed the flock of God,"* from this time when Jesus had questioned him. Jesus used the word "lamb" in verse 15, and "sheep" in verses 16 and 17. Jesus was making a distinction. There is an obvious difference between a lamb, which is a baby or newborn, and a sheep, which is an adult.

The Greek word for "feed" in verse 15 is *bosko*, and it means exactly that, to feed. But the Greek word translated "feed" in verses 16 and 17 is *poimen*, which means to pastor.

Jesus was making a very important point. When being fed, a newborn lamb must have a bottle placed in its mouth. But full-grown sheep are led by the shepherd to a grassy area to eat. The shepherd does not feed the adult sheep, they must eat on their own.

The local church is to care for both the newborns and the adults. Oftentimes, a church will cater to one or the other. For example, in some churches many people are born again, but provide nothing to feed the babies or challenge the adults so they can all grow and mature.

Some pastors preach an evangelistic message every Sunday and Wednesday, but never teach the Word of God. Other pastors only offer the *"solid food"* or meat of the Word for the spiritual adults in their congregations. When I pastored, foundational classes were offered for new believers. While I was teaching the meat of the Word in the regular service, the spiritual babies were receiving the *"milk"* of the Word. (See Hebrews 5:12-14.)

Like babies in the natural, new believers need a more intimate time to drink the milk of the Word and require attention that is more personal. But when they come into the main services, they will begin to take tiny bites of the meat of God's Word.

At first they will leave shaking their heads, digesting only small portions of what they are fed. But as they begin to grow, you will observe changes in their lives. The Word will take hold in their hearts. Stability and wisdom will be seen.

If there is no growth, a problem exists. If a full-grown sheep is needing a bottle, something is wrong with that sheep! You wouldn't put teenagers in a highchair and feed them baby food. Believers have a responsibility. After you give them the Word, they must choose to believe it and live it.

Unless you are located in a very sparsely populated area, you should always have new converts in a church. I have found, regardless of the topic I would teach, the Holy Spirit would almost always weave in an evangelistic message during the sermon. This would lead to an invitation for people to be saved, filled with the Holy Spirit, or restored to fellowship.

Perhaps you have heard people say, "Jesus is coming back for a church without spot or wrinkle" (Ephesians 5:25-27). Some use this verse incorrectly, implying the church must be perfect before Jesus returns. If that is the case, He is never coming back because we will never be perfect as long as new babies are coming into the kingdom and carnal Christians exist who are filled with spots and wrinkles!

If this interpretation of this scripture were correct, we would have to stop getting people born again and just work on ourselves for Jesus to come back for us! The apostle Paul said, *"I do not count myself to have apprehended..."* [to lay hold of or fully appropriate every benefit of salvation] (Philippians 3:13). If the apostle Paul made this statement, what makes us think we will ever become perfected in this life?

Full maturity will not occur in the family of God until we all get to heaven. There, *"He might present her* [us] *to Himself a glorious church, not having spot or wrinkle..."* (Ephesians 5:27). Only after the judgment seat of Christ will we reach the unity of the faith and the full measure of the stature of Christ (Ephesians 4:13).

Until then, how do you pastor all these growing, hungry lambs and sheep? Simply give them everything the Holy Spirit gives you from the Word. Make sure the babies are getting the milk of the Word, and all the sheep, young and old, are offered the meat of the Word.

As with natural food, when you learn about a "new recipe," add it in. Why? You are adding variety and flavor to the food to make it more appealing. I am not advocating that you develop unscriptural and foolish sermons just to entertain your congregation. But if God leads you to teach something in a special way, do it.

Have you ever noticed when you go to a restaurant, the way the food is served makes it either more or less appealing? And the atmosphere of the restaurant also makes a big difference in your ability to enjoy the food. That is where praise and worship come in. God inhabits the praises of His people, and the presence of God is the atmosphere in which the sheep will best eat.

Some people may not find the atmosphere (music ministry) or the way the food is served (teaching of the Word) at your church to their taste. That is why God gives individual pastors a vision specific to an area or group of people.

Just as different people prefer different types of restaurants, members of the body of Christ prefer different ways to worship. Although we may be worshipping the same God, and preaching and teaching the same Bible, the presentation is different from church to church. It is the same food, but it is prepared differently.

I have found most great pastors today have grown up in the area in which they are called to pastor. When I was a teacher at a Bible training school, first-year students would come through the door declaring, "I'll never go back home!" But by graduation, God had given them a desire to take what they had learned back to their hometown.

When you grow up in an area, you know how the people think, what they like and dislike, and how they communicate. You can use examples they can identify with—you know how to prepare the Word of God so it will look good, taste good, and digest more easily! In Colossians 4:12, Paul mentioned the pastor of the Colossians church, *"Epaphras, who is* one of you."

Peter's ministry was to the Jews because his whole life's experience was among the Jewish people. And I believe one of the reasons God chose Paul to minister to the Gentiles was because Paul was a Roman citizen. He had a working knowledge of Gentile thinking and culture.

But whether the pastor is one of their own or not, it is important for a congregation to know their pastor understands what they are going through. That he is preaching and teaching the Word of God to help them live productive, fulfilled lives. In this way, they can boldly and confidently face the challenges of the day and be effective witnesses for Jesus in their city.

THE PASTOR'S GREATEST ASSET

Some pastors get the idea they have the power in the church. In reality, the people are the true power of the church. God can very easily replace pastors, but it is more difficult to replace whole congregations! Many congregations have continued to exist for long periods of time without a pastor, but no church can exist without a congregation.

The greatest asset the pastor has is not the buildings or the offerings. Neither is it his preaching nor teaching ability. His greatest asset is the people, and he must always remember he will be held accountable for how he treats the flock of God.

Some pastors beat their sheep from the pulpit, and then wonder why the flock scatters. Whenever anything goes wrong or there's not enough money, they always blame the people.

There may be times when the congregation is at fault in some area, and the pastor may be led by the Spirit of God to exhort and instruct them. But his responsibility, in these situations, is to deal with the problem by exhorting the people in the Word of God and encouraging them to grow up spiritually (2 Timothy 3:16-17). He should correct and instruct with love and wisdom, not guilt and condemnation.

Constant bombardment of guilt and condemnation will not edify and motivate people to change. This only causes the sheep to scatter. God will not allow His children to be beaten this way for long. He will lead them to a pastor who practices "grace thinking" (see Chapter 2), who will love them as God does and feed them well.

God has appointed the pastor to lead, feed, and protect His most precious possession—His people. This is an awesome responsibility. The devil would wake me up at four o'clock in the morning and say, "You have all of those people and all of those problems and all of those needs! What are you going to do? How can you possibly do it all?"

I would start thinking, *I don't know! Lord, what am I going to do?*

But the Lord answers, "They are not your sheep, Bob! Just do what I have told you to do, by My Spirit and My Word, and let Me handle the rest."

For example, Jethro hired Moses to watch his sheep; and Jesse had his son, David, watch over his sheep. Pastors do not own their sheep either!

Shepherds should never tell their sheep, "You're my sheep and you have to stay with me." No, the sheep go where the owner leads them. They submit themselves to the shepherd under whom the owner places them.

All shepherds are working for the Owner, Jesus Christ, the Chief Shepherd. Through the Holy Spirit, He will guide them where to pastor. Then He will bring sheep to them, to lead and feed as He directs. A pastor does not need to strive to make his congregation grow or hold people in his church.

Neither should the pastor turn his congregation into his disciples. Instead, he is to teach the people how to be disciples of Jesus Christ. Discipleship becomes error when those in the pulpit teach that you are to become a disciple to them.

Some pastors go overboard by taking too great an interest in the individual lives of their congregational members. It is good for a pastor to care for his people and have a general knowledge of what they are facing. However, it should not matter to him the kind of cars they drive, where they live, or how many children they have.

It is not the pastor's responsibility to go to the homes of his people to check up on them, to make sure they are living what he preached last Sunday. Nor should he direct the elders of the church to do this.

The pastor's duty is to give the Word of God to the people. To hold nothing back, and to teach the whole counsel of God. He should point them to Jesus, the Owner and Chief Shepherd. The pastor should prepare the Word and make it as appealing as possible, presenting it in an atmosphere filled with the presence of God—beginning with praise and worship. Each individual then has a choice as to whether or not they receive and live the Word that has been taught.

Chapter 9

TAKING AUTHORITY

Shepherd the flock of God which is among you, serving as overseers, not by compulsion but willingly, not for dishonest gain but eagerly; nor as being lords over those entrusted to you, but being examples to the flock (1 Peter 5:2-3).

Even though the sheep do not belong to you, the Word of God declares you, as pastor, are *"serving as overseers."* This means you are to take your God-given authority, stand in it, and make decisions that are yours alone to make. God will not hand it to you; He commands *you* to take it.

You ask, "But what if I make a wrong decision?" You will find out soon enough. Simply go back and make the right decision! The point is, if *you* don't make a decision, somebody else will.

You say, "But I just don't want to make waves." It's a fact—you *will* make waves! Most people find change difficult to handle, and sometime cages get rattled when you determine to do God's will. But it is much better to make some waves and do the will of God than to timidly sit back and try to please people.

In Acts 20:28, the Word of God declares that *"the Holy Spirit has made you overseers."* If the Holy Spirit has made you an overseer, then when you take the oversight, He will reveal the direction you are to go, day by day, decision by decision. He knows the end from the beginning, and nothing takes Him by surprise!

God places the pastor in the office of chief overseer of the local church, which means He gives him the vision for that church. It is the pastor who knows the direction the church should be going. Nothing is worse than a leader who does not lead.

But when the pastor says, "This is the vision. This is what we are supposed to do," and he begins to delegate responsibilities, everybody will respond to his leadership and follow through. Why? Because the pastor is taking the oversight. He is using the ruling authority God commands him to use, and the people will take hold of that boldness and rest in the security that comes when they know he is doing God's will.

A WILLING SERVANT

No one forces you to be a pastor. Instead, you are *"taking the oversight thereof, not by constraint* [coercion], *but willingly..."* (1 Peter 5:2-3 KJV). What Paul explained is that pastors should never do anything because of pressure or coercion.

Many places I go, there is usually a pastor who says, "I just don't understand it! My church isn't growing. People don't like me. I'm preaching the Word, I'm praying, and my family life is good. But the church is a failure."

I ask them, "How did you come to this church?" They usually respond with something similar to, "Well, I came to a small prayer group, and they prophesied over me that I was supposed to be the pastor. Then they just kept asking me and asking me until I finally said I would take the church." Or they might say, "I came here because the people believed I was their pastor. They voted me in 100 percent!"

Don't ever agree to take a position because of pressure from people. Take it because God told you. If they have already waited two or three years for a pastor, they can wait for God to confirm and give you peace about whether or not to take a position. Having 100 percent of the vote does not mean the vote is God's will. The only way you can pastor willingly is by knowing it is God's will—not the misguided will of others for you.

A pastor once told me he didn't like pastoring, but God had "forced" him into it. This was his "cross to bear." Every day he would "pick up his cross" and go to the church.

Your ministry is not your cross to bear! There may be difficult experiences and times when you have to crucify your flesh to be faithful and diligent to study and pray, but you still know God has called you. When God calls you to a ministry, He drops a desire for it in your heart. He doesn't call you to something you hate in order to teach you something, nor does He look down at you from heaven and laugh as you blunder through it. No! That is not God!

God will give you a deep desire to see His will fulfilled in your life and in the lives of those He has called you to serve. The ministry He calls you to will be an outward reflection and fulfillment of that desire. It is true that it will bring some of your greatest challenges, but it will also bring times of the greatest rewards.

FREEDOM TO SERVE

First Peter 5:2 continues, *"...not for dishonest gain but eagerly...."* Never take a church because the salary looks good either! That is another way of missing God. You may be rich financially, but miserable in every other area. Take the church because God tells you to take it, and do not make any stipulation about your salary. There is nothing wrong about asking what your salary will be. Or negotiating. But if the church doesn't supply your needs, trust God to fill the deficiency.

Understand that money is good, not evil; it is *"the love of money that is the root of all evil"* (1 Timothy 6:10). Whether you are in business, a minister, or a housewife, you can have *"dishonest gain,"* or an evil, covetous attitude toward money.

The Word of God says that the right attitude toward money is to *"remember the Lord your God, for it is He that gives you power to get wealth, that He may establish His covenant which He swore to your fathers, as it is this day"* (Deuteronomy 8:18).

God will prosper you and give you money because He trusts you to know what to do with it. He knows you won't just keep it all for yourself, but will give into the gospel. Because establishing His covenant on earth is first and foremost in your mind. Do not love money.

Love God and use the money to spread the gospel. I traveled before I became a pastor and I met ministers who would not go to a church unless they were guaranteed a specified amount of money. There are many churches that may be unable to bring you in because of their current financial situation. But if it is God's will for you to minister at that church, He will provide the difference.

I went to one church and spent more money traveling to and from the meeting than I had received as an offering. But the next Sunday, someone in my home church slipped $500 in my hand and said, "God told me to give this to you." If you are obedient to the Holy Spirit and resist financial pressure, He will see you through!

I have also known some pastors who treat churches as steppingstones in some grand career path they have set for themselves. They will resign one church and go to another just because the pay is better.

Every position the Lord places you in should be treated as the ultimate for you. If you are the janitor of the church and God has called you to keep the building clean, you should be content and know He will supply all your needs. You should be the happiest, most prosperous janitor in the world because you know you are in His will.

As a pastor, trust God to meet your needs, no matter how small or large, rich or poor your congregation may be. The Bible says to *"seek first the kingdom of God and His righteousness, and all these things shall be added to you"* (Matthew 6:33).

I would rather be in God's will receiving a small salary than out of His will making millions! Money cannot buy you peace, contentment, or fulfillment. If God has called you to a church, He has not called you there to fail. Depend on Him to supply your needs as you faithfully continue preaching and teaching His Word and carrying out His vision for that church.

DON'T MUZZLE THE OX

Sometimes church members read *"...not for dishonest gain,"* and they think, "We don't want our pastor to be puffed up in pride, so we aren't going to pay him much." Ironically, this is contrary to what the Word of God says. In 1 Timothy 5:17-18, Paul gave an exhortation to Timothy, *"Let the elders who rule well be counted worthy of double honor, especially those who labor in the word and doctrine. For the Scripture says, 'You shall not muzzle an ox while it treads out the grain,' and, 'The laborer is worthy of his wages.'"*

This passage of scripture is directed to those who control the pastor's salary. It is usually a board of elders in the church. Unless the church is very small, the pastor should *not* set his own salary.

When the church has grown large enough and the pastor knows the members well enough to appoint those who have proven themselves faithful to the Word of God, he should appoint a governing board under him. This provides a practical check and balance system in three specific areas:

1. Taking appropriate action if the pastor should fall into sin, such as adultery.
2. Providing a source of godly counsel for the pastor.
3. Most importantly, releasing the pastor from setting his own salary.

Those who *"labor in the word and doctrine"* are the pastors, and the phrase *"double honor"* is specifically referring to money. *"Double honor"* means double pay. Many people think double honor should be a couple of good pats on the back instead of one! But verse 18 is a quote from Deuteronomy 25:4, which is speaking about finances.

In the ancient world, the ox was tied up so it could walk around in a circle all day and tread out the corn. The farmer, who wanted to keep as much corn as possible, would put a muzzle on the ox to prevent it from dipping its head to eat what was thrown on the threshing floor. But the Old Testament commanded Israel to treat their animals well. The ox was *not* to be muzzled.

The corn represents finances, and the ox is the pastor, locked up in his office, going around and around all day: studying, praying, preaching; studying, praying, preaching; studying, praying, preaching!

The Word of God says you shouldn't put a muzzle on the pastor. Let him *"be counted worthy of double honor…for the laborer is worthy of his wages."* This is saying that being a pastor is not only a calling, it is an occupation. Studying, praying, and preaching is the way he earns his living.

Often, assistants in secular businesses earn more than pastors. Many churches do not want their pastor to "dip down" to take any money, so they muzzle him. However, this is contrary to the Word. *God wants the church to understand that pastoring is not a pastime!* It is just as much a full-time job as being a welder or a doctor.

When you take a church, do not take it because of the salary. If money is your reason for taking the church, you become bound to the church *and* to your salary because of the money. There is only one reason to take a church—because the Lord has called you to that church.

When you take a church because God told you to take it, you place yourself in His hands and you can minister *"of a ready mind."* In other words, you can minister freely. As the Holy Spirit directs, teach your congregation what the Word has to say about those *"who labor in the word and doctrine."* Most congregations are so grateful to receive the Word week after week, they want to bless their pastor in any way they are able. Especially toward his income.

THE BALANCE OF AUTHORITY

There is a balance in 1 Peter 5:2-3 (KJV) to *"taking the oversight...neither as being lords over God's heritage, but being examples to the flock."* In essence, Peter told the pastors they could be head of the church without being a dictator.

When I became pastor of our church, the first thing I studied and taught was church government. In all my years in the church, I had observed very few church government situations that were positive. I wanted to learn what the Bible had to say about the subject.

One of the most widespread problems I witnessed involved pastors who had to do what a board of elders or a superintendent told him to do. In some cases, he even had to teach the congregation what *they* thought should be taught!

I found and began to teach from God's Word that the pastor is the head of the local church, just as Jesus is the Head of the universal Church. A few cried out, "Dictator!" But most were grateful to have a pastor who took the oversight.

If God had not placed pastors as head of the local church, it would be unnecessary for the Holy Spirit to warn pastors against being dictators. He admonishes pastors not to abuse the ruling authority that rightfully comes with their position as an overseer of a local church.

I once received a letter from someone accusing me of setting myself up as a dictator over the church. This individual had read my book on church government— *Decently and in Order*—and said I was in error when I said the pastor receives his authority directly from the Lord Jesus Christ.

They argued that because the fivefold ministry gifts are listed in the order of apostles, prophets, evangelists, pastors, and teachers (Ephesians 4:11), the pastor should submit himself to those above him. Ultimately, they explained to me their belief that each local church should have a prophet and an apostle, based on Ephesians 2:20, where it states that the church is *"built on the foundation of the apostles and prophets, Jesus Christ Himself, being the chief cornerstone."*

But the question then arises, "Who does the apostle submit to? Does he become a dictator?" Ephesians 2:20 is not declaring apostles and prophets *themselves* are the foundation. This verse is saying our churches should be built upon the same foundation of the apostle and prophets, the writers of the Word of God—*"Jesus Christ being the chief cornerstone."*

Neither is Ephesians 4:11 setting a chain of command among the fivefold ministry gifts. The Holy Spirit is simply telling us the chronological order in which God gave these gifts to the Church.

The first office given after the day of Pentecost was the apostle who established the local church at Jerusalem (Acts 2:42). Next came the prophets and the first evangelist (Acts 8). The last offices to be placed, as local churches were being established, were pastors and teachers (Acts 14:23).

Clearly, each individual office receives their authority directly from Jesus Christ. Otherwise, the scripture would read, "And he gave some, apostles; and the apostles gave some, prophets; and the prophets gave some, evangelists, etc." This verse says *Jesus* gave each gift.

Also, in these verses of scripture, Peter and Paul, who were both apostles, did not formally set themselves above the other pastors and elders. In each case, they emphasized they had come to exhort and encourage the pastors as *"fellow elders"* and *"fellow ministers."*

In other words, Peter and Paul are not telling the pastors *how* to run their churches. They are teaching them the Word of God and imparting practical wisdom and sound guidelines that will enable these pastors to *oversee* the churches themselves.

There is nothing in the Bible that indicates the pastor should look to anyone but the Lord Jesus Christ for final authority and direction for the church he pastors. He should receive much counsel and wisdom from those around him. But, once he prayerfully considers their input, his final authority is the Lord.

> *Shepherd the flock of God which is among you, serving as overseers, not by compulsion but willingly, not for dishonest gain but eagerly; nor as being lords over those entrusted to you, but being examples to the flock* (1 Peter 5:3).

At the same time, in 1 Peter 5:3, the Holy Spirit exhorts pastors not to abuse their authority: "...*nor as being lords over those entrusted to you...*" (notice Who has entrusted the congregation to you) "*but being examples to the flock.*" Your people will never see you as a dictator if you live what you preach and teach. Those who act as dictators over their congregations are not doers of the Word they preach.

Your life should merely be an extension of the pulpit; the pulpit should be an extension of your life. You should be the same in the pulpit and out of the pulpit. You should run your home the same way you run the church (1 Timothy 3:5).

Your ministry doesn't begin in the pulpit; it begins when you get up in the morning! A minister is not something you *do*—it is something you *are*. As an example to the flock, the pastor should do his best to live what he teaches. Ministers are not to point to the Word of God and then live any way they feel like living!

There is nothing wrong with using yourself as an example from time to time.—if you guard yourself against pride. Paul used himself as an example many times throughout the New Testament, including Acts 20:20: *"how I have kept back nothing that was helpful, but proclaimed it to you, and taught you publicly and from house to house."*

VOLUNTARY SLAVERY

A very interesting little-used Greek word for "minister" is *huperetes*. It actually means an "underrower." It is used in Acts 13:5 (KJV) to describe Mark, who traveled with Paul and Barnabas on their first missionary journey.

In the time in which Paul lived, there were three different levels of rowers on a Roman ship, and all the rowers were slaves. It may not edify you greatly to hear that as a minister you are a slave, but the ministry is not all glamorous; it can be hard work! When you choose to be a minister, you choose to become a slave to the Lord Jesus Christ.

In 2 Peter 1:1, Peter makes a point of declaring he is first a servant, or literally a bondslave, and second, an apostle of Jesus Christ. By referring to himself as a bondslave, Peter is declaring he has voluntarily sold his entire life to Jesus. He has no personal rights, privileges, or property. Everything he has, is, or does belongs to his Lord.

Likewise, Paul and Timothy, in addressing the Philippians (Philippians 1:1) call themselves the *"bond-servants* [bondslaves] *of Jesus Christ."* Literally, they are saying they are Jesus' property (Romans 1:1; Titus 1:1).

Anyone who is born again automatically becomes a child of God, but a believer chooses whether they will become a slave, completely committed to Jesus. A minister, by definition, has chosen to become a permanent slave for the Lord.

Rowers on the upper levels of the ship could row more easily because the oars barely dipped below the surface of the water. But the lower the level the underrower was located on the ship, the more difficult it was to row because the oars dipped more deeply into the water.

It is obvious, those who have the most enjoyable time on the boat are the ones who sit on deck and just enjoy the breeze and the sun. This is the congregation! They sit during Sunday and midweek services and enjoy the Word and the presence of God because all week the pastor and his helpers have been underrowers.

ESTABLISHING A RELATIONSHIP

When I became pastor of our church, my wife and I had already been active members from the very first service of the church under the founding pastor. Nearly everyone in the congregation was familiar with us because I had taught classes and had even taught from the pulpit on a regular basis. By the time God placed me in the position of pastor, a strong relationship between the people and me had already been established. This enabled me to almost immediately begin teaching on proper church government and walking in the responsibility God gave me from His Word, which belonged to me as pastor of the church.

But most pastors, whether they are beginning a new church or are taking over a church someone else has pastored, have the task of establishing a relationship with the people before they can take full authority. A pastor forms a relationship with his people and ultimately establishes his authority by showing them who he is and by faithfully teaching the Word of God.

Regardless of how difficult or negative the situation may be when you become pastor, take enough time to let the people know you and get used to your delivery of the Word of God before you begin making changes. When you first come to a church, your authority is not the issue—*you* are the issue! Authority will be received when the people know you and trust you; it cannot be forced.

After you have established a relationship, then you can begin the process of slowly setting policies as you teach the congregation what the Word of God has to say about the office of a pastor and church government. Clean the house slowly and prayerfully.

If there are some difficult or even corrupt people on staff or in positions of authority, draw upon the grace of God to minister to them and to give you patience until the situations turn around or the Holy Spirit releases you to replace them. But establish the relationship *first*.

Be careful not to let those you socialize with dictate policy to you either. When you are out with friends from the church, gently make it clear you do not mix business with pleasure. Some may be offended at first, because they may have invited you to lunch to discuss "their agenda." But the congregation will ultimately find security in the fact their pastor is not dictated to by his friends.

Another issue to be aware of is not to let your wife dictate policy through you. She is your helper and counsel. You should talk things over with her and receive her input in the same way you would receive counsel from close friends.

However, just as you should not start up a church *"by constraint,"* or because of pressure from people, neither should you *"run"* the church by the pressure of people. Your authority comes from the Lord Jesus Christ, and He is the One who will ultimately lead you.

Along these same lines, you should protect your wife and family from the church. Do not allow members of the congregation to get to you through your wife or your children. Family time is family time. This is not the time to discuss church business. Keep your family informed about what is going on so they won't be surprised if someone shares something they should already know about. But assure them church business will be handled by you at the church.

Right from the beginning, if you are not accustomed to confrontation or have avoided dealing with conflict in the past, get in the habit of confronting people directly and privately. Some pastors avoid confrontation with one individual or a few members by preaching against them from the pulpit. This is the coward's way to handle conflict. Instead, go to them and settle the issue privately.

When a pastor either avoids these issues or discovers gossip is spreading through the congregation, he will be forced to address the problem from the pulpit, because it has affected too many people.

Some pastors are actually afraid to take the oversight—to firmly grasp the ministry God has given them and take the reins, because they fear somebody will say they are a dictator. That is like a father saying, "I'm not going to run this family. I don't want my wife and kids to think I'm a dictator." Believe me, the kids are waiting for you to take the reins. Your wife is waiting for you to make a decision, and the world wants you to take charge of your family!

Many people mistake being confident in authority for arrogance. Arrogant people are self-made; confident people are God-made. When you are confident, all the glory goes to God. You can step into the pulpit and preach and teach His Word in power, knowing it is the

Word and the Holy Spirit working in you. If you realize it is God's ability and not your own working in you, you *will* succeed!

Know where your confidence is. God called you to pastor this church. He will give you the grace to establish a strong relationship with the people. He commands you to *"take the oversight,"* and He will give you the strength and wisdom to fulfill your calling.

Throughout the Word of God, the church is compared to two things: a body and a family. A body and a family each have one head. One who is given ruling authority. In the body of Christ, Jesus is the Head; and in the family, the husband has final authority and accountability for his family.

In the local church, the pastor is commanded to take the oversight, and he is the one who labors more in the Word of God than anyone else in his church. He is to be a faithful example to his flock. If he does these things, he will not become a dictator or *"lord over God's heritage."* He will take the oversight with compassion and integrity as God commands.

Chapter 10

THE CHIEF SHEPHERD SHALL APPEAR

And when the Chief Shepherd appears, you will receive the crown of glory that does not fade away (1 Peter 5:4).

Jesus embodied all of the fivefold ministry gifts. Hebrews 3:1 calls Him *"the Apostle and High Priest of our confession."* In Acts 3:22-23, Peter calls Him *"a Prophet."* From the Gospel accounts, it is obvious He preached and did the work of an evangelist. And Nicodemus called Him *"a teacher come from God"* in John 3:2. But now in 1 Peter 5:4, Jesus is referred to as the *"Chief Shepherd,"* or we could say Chief Pastor.

God did not pressure or coerce Jesus into becoming our *"Chief Shepherd."* He did it *"willingly, not by constraint"* (1 Peter 5:2 KJV). Neither did Jesus become Head of the Church because He was offered a tremendous salary! In fact, He gave up everything He owned to come and redeem us. Therefore, He was free to do God's will, and God supplied all of His needs.

Although Jesus has been given all authority in heaven and earth, He is not a dictator over the body of Christ. He allows us to choose whether or not we will follow Him, and He is the supreme example for us to follow.

SOMEONE TO TURN TO

When Peter makes reference to the *"Chief Shepherd,"* he is reminding these pastors they also have a Pastor who is always with them. Pastors will sometimes ask me, "Will you be my pastor?" I consider that a great honor. There are also times when I will call other pastors for advice and counsel.

But even if you have been called to the most remote area imaginable, and wish you could seek advice from a pastor, always remember you can! His name is Jesus! He is the Chief Pastor, and He is always there. You will never find Him out of the office, away on an emergency, or having left instructions with the Holy Spirit that He is not to be disturbed.

In Hebrews 13:20, Jesus is called the *"great Shepherd of the sheep,"* and He is called *"the Word"* in John 1:1,14. Therefore, as He feeds you, you in turn can feed the congregation.

People often ask, "Can I use your sermons to teach others?" What they don't realize is they are not my sermons. In fact, it is possible that portions of my message came from the recordings and books of other ministers I have studied. And in reality, if you asked those ministers where they got their messages, they would probably admit portions of their messages came from other ministers as well!

We can use what God has given others because any revelation they have received has come from the Lord. As you read books, listen to recordings, and meditate on the Word prayerfully, the Holy Spirit will make the truth real to you. When it becomes real to you it becomes your own revelation.

Personally, I believe it is wrong to ignore the materials where others have already received revelation on a topic and expect the Holy Spirit to give you "special" revelation on the same topic. Revelation is built upon revelation. If you refuse to read good books and listen to sermons, the Holy Spirit is not bound to "reinvent the wheel." It is when you study what He has already revealed to others that He is faithful to reveal more to your heart.

However, using someone else's material alone is not enough either. While in our bookstore one day, a couple of visiting pastors were talking. One asked the other, "What reference materials do you use most of the time?" Our bookstore manager was horrified to hear the response, "Oh, I just listen to a message on Saturday night and preach it on Sunday morning!"

This is not only an injustice to the congregation, but to the pastor himself. It is good to listen to recordings and read books, but meditate on the material and the Word you are studying long enough to make the message your own. *"Be diligent to present yourself approved to God, a worker who does not need to be ashamed..."* (2 Timothy 2:15).

THE ALPHA AND THE OMEGA

In Revelation 1:9, the apostle John wrote, *"I, John, both your brother and companion in tribulation...."* Like Paul and Peter, he didn't emphasize the fact he was an apostle, rather that he was a fellow servant and minister of Jesus Christ.

In Revelation 1:10 and 11, John continues:

> *I was in the Spirit on the Lord's Day, and I heard behind me a loud voice, as of a trumpet, saying, "I am the Alpha and the Omega, the First and the Last," and, "What you see, write in a book and send it to the seven churches which are in Asia: to Ephesus, to Smyrna, to Pergamos, to Thyatira, to Sardis, to Philadelphia, and to Laodicea."*

The greatest pastor in the whole world had come to visit John! In verse 12 he says, *"Then I turned to see the voice that spoke with me. And having turned, I saw seven golden lampstands."* The seven lampstands refer to the seven churches mentioned in verse 11.

In those days, a lampstand was not a little holder with a wax candle in it. Instead, they were lamps filled with oil. Each church is represented by an oil lamp and the oil represents the Holy Spirit. God is saying churches are to be filled with the light of the Holy Spirit, shining brightly in the darkness of this world.

Revelation 1:13 continues, *"And in the midst* [literally, walking around in the midst] *of the seven lampstands One like the Son of Man, clothed with a garment down to the feet and girded about the chest with a golden band."* This, of course, refers to Jesus, our High Priest. It says He was clothed magnificently with a robe down to His feet and a golden band, or breastplate, around His chest.

In the Old Testament, the high priest wore a breastplate with twelve stones, representing the twelve tribes of Israel. But the one that Jesus is wearing does not have the stones because He is acting as the High Priest over the Church. John was watching our High Priest and Chief Shepherd of the Church walk among these seven local churches.

I want you to understand what these verses of scripture are revealing to us about Jesus today. In this passage, He is not just the meek, mild Jesus who came to earth and was laid in the manger. These verses paint a picture of our risen Lord Jesus who has ascended on high and has been seated at the right hand of the Father—King of kings and Lord of lords over heaven and earth! And this is also a description of the same Jesus who is walking among the churches today!

Jesus is not walking among dead, religious churches either. He is walking among living, powerful churches that are truly lamps in this world, bringing the truth of God's Word and power to the lost and needy. He is walking in the midst of your church today as you preach and teach the Word of God and are led in and by the power of the Holy Spirit.

Revelation 1:14 continues, *"His head and hair were white like wool, as white as snow,"* which symbolizes His sinless, righteous character, *"and His eyes like a flame of fire,"* which shows nothing escapes His vision.

Verse 15: *"His feet were like fine brass, as if refined in a furnace,"* which refers to judgment, *"and His voice as the sound of many waters."* Can you imagine trying to hear yourself talk when standing at the bottom of Niagara Falls? When Jesus Christ speaks, you cannot even try to object, because His Word is the final authority and will drown you out completely.

Verse 16: *"He had in His right hand seven stars...."* These represent the seven pastors of the seven churches. We know this, because in verse 20 Jesus told John, *"The mystery of the seven stars which you saw in My right hand, and the seven golden lampstands: The seven stars are the angels of the seven churches, and the seven lampstands which you saw are the seven churches."*

Most people believe, based on this verse of scripture, each local church must have an angel assigned to it. I don't know if that is true or not, but I can tell you verse 20 is not speaking of an angel from heaven.

The Greek word for "angel" is *angelos*. However, in most cases in Greek literature, it is not used to refer to an angel, but rather to a messenger, whether from men or from God.

In James 2:25, the Bible says Rahab the harlot received the *"messengers"* with peace. The messengers or the two spies who were sent out are called *angelos* in the Greek.

Since *angelos* can mean messengers that God sends (either men or angels), or messengers that men send, how do we know whether verse 20 is talking about divine angels from heaven or human beings?

> *To the angel of the church of Ephesus write, "These things says He who holds the seven stars in His right hand, who walks in the midst of the seven golden lampstands: 'I know your works, your labor, your patience, and that you cannot bear those who are evil. And you have tested those who say they are apostles and are not and have found them liars; and you have persevered and have patience, and have labored for My name's sake and have not become weary. Nevertheless, I have this against you, that you have left your first love'"* (Revelation 2:1-4).

In this letter, and in all of the seven letters in chapters 2 and 3 of Revelation, Jesus addressed *"the angel"* or *"the messenger*" of that local church. But wait! We know this can't be an angel from heaven because no angel has left their first love. If they had, they would no longer be serving God!

Jesus is addressing the human messengers whom He sent to oversee these churches—the pastors. In each letter, He has something against the messenger, the pastor, placed over each church. He lets them know the areas that please Him and those that disappoint Him. He also commends those areas in which they are succeeding and exhorts them about those areas needing change. Jesus holds the pastor accountable for the spiritual growth and maturity of the local church.

I also want you to notice there was only one angel, or pastor, over each church. God recognizes one pastor for each of the seven churches. And the seven stars, which Jesus indicated were the pastors of the seven churches (Revelation 1:20), were not in John's hand or another apostle's hand; they were not in a prophet's hand; they were in the hand of the Lord Jesus Christ.

Each believer's ministry comes from the Lord Jesus, and we are each accountable to Him. We may answer to others around us, but our ministry office comes only from Jesus, and we are in His hand of power and protection.

His Eyes Are a Flame of Fire

Jesus walks among the churches today, which means He walks among all believers. Remember as He walks in your congregation, His eyes are a penetrating flame of fire, and nothing gets past Him. These eyes see past the outward life into the motive of the heart, where sin begins (Hebrews 4:13).

Jesus sees into the heart of every believer, but He holds the pastor accountable for the spiritual well-being of the church. First Peter 5:3 says the pastor is to be an example to the flock, and in Revelation, chapters 1 through 3, it is to the pastors of the churches Jesus speaks when He comes to encourage and correct the churches. The call to the ministry means the pastor lives by a higher standard than the congregation. God holds him to a greater accountability (James 3:1).

Because of this greater accountability, the sins you commit in private, God will make public. This may not include things you do accidentally or things for which you have repented and received forgiveness. This is whatever sins you persist in doing. If you live a double standard, preach one way, and live another way, God will see to it that it is exposed.

The reason God acts so strongly in this area is because in whatever sins the pastor indulges, that same sin will be found in his congregation. A church reflects the personality and life of its pastor. What he allows in his life, the people will allow in theirs.

Just as Jesus is the door for the universal Church (John 10:7), the pastor is the door for the local church. He is the door allowing blessing or cursing into the flock. When there is righteousness in the pulpit, there will be righteousness in the congregation. If there is immorality in the pulpit, there will be immorality in the congregation.

We have seen sheep are God's precious possession and ultimately His responsibility. Therefore, He will not tolerate a wayward pastor for His people for any length of time. God is long suffering, but not infinite suffering!

I am not referring to small problem areas—every church has those and must deal with them. These problems are not necessarily a reflection of the pastorate. But when a certain sin pervades most of the congregation, it is usually because the pastor is having the same problem. Because he refuses to plug the holes in his own life with the Word, the devil will use those openings as doorways into the congregation.

No pastor perfectly lives everything he preaches and teaches. And it is wrong for the congregation to expect the pastor to be perfect, but they can expect him to be faithful, to be an example to follow, and the chief one among them to practice what he teaches. They can expect him to live a moral, godly life before them and the world.

Sin is always selfish. I am ever amazed when a minister admits to sinning, while at the same time acknowledging he never thought about how his sin would hurt his family, friends, church, or the body of Christ at large. Whether it is a short time of pleasure or what appears to be an easy way out of a difficult situation, in the end, your sin will cause immeasurable damage to those you love.

As believers, we are repeatedly exhorted to guard our hearts against the wiles of the devil to entrap us in sin. The way we guard our hearts is by the Word of God. Therefore, as the one who feeds the sheep, the pastor of the flock should have the greatest hedge of protection around his own heart.

Psalm 119:11 says, *"Your word I have hidden in my heart...."* And 2 Peter 1:4 says, *"By which have been given to us exceedingly great and precious promises, that through these you may be partakers of the divine nature, having escaped the corruption that is in the world through lust."*

If a pastor sins in a major area and truly repents, the board of advisors, deacons, or elders of the church should determine a period of time before he will return to the pulpit. It has taken time for the pastor to fall into sin, and it will take time for him to renew his mind with God's Word to build new habits of thinking and behavior to replace the wrong ones.

In some cases, the hurt and outrage of the congregation may be so great it will be impossible for the pastor to return. However, if he truly repents and submits himself to another pastor's authority until he is fully restored, he should continue to fulfill his calling. Other than Jesus, no hero of faith in the Word of God was a hero because they were perfect. They were a hero because they got back up after they failed.

If a pastor goes into error or is overtaken in a fault and does not repent, the advisory board or board of elders should have the authority to fire him. In our church, this was the practical balance of authority: the pastor chooses the members of the advisory board, but the advisory board has authority over his salary and even his position in cases of extreme sin or doctrinal heresy.

But whatever the checks and balances are in your church government, pastors must always remember Jesus will have the final word! The pastor is called the star, but Jesus is the Sun, shining in full strength; the pastor is a voice, but Jesus is the living Word who speaks as many waters. His voice can never be overpowered or silenced, no matter what a pastor may say or do.

A life of holiness is expected and demanded by our Lord Jesus. Get rid of the image of an overindulgent Jesus who will let you brush off sin and ignore the things you are doing! He is merciful and gracious to *"forgive us our sins and to cleanse us from all unrighteousness"* (1 John 1:9), but don't think He doesn't care if we sin. His eyes are a flame of fire!

THE PASTOR'S CROWN

Salvation is a gift, but rewards will be given in heaven for the works we do on this earth in line with God's will for our individual lives (Revelation 14:13). The Bible talks about many different rewards in heaven, and specifically mentions a number of golden crowns.

In the Greek culture, the crown was actually a wreath made of olive leaves. The one who received the wreath was the person who won the race. But there will be more than one winner in heaven! Jesus will be handing out many wreaths made of gold that won't fade away. The rewards won't be limited to one gold medal, one silver medal, and one bronze medal as we have today in the Olympic games. The gold will be available to everyone who finishes their race.

Many believers will just make it into heaven (1 Corinthians 3:15). But I want to earn many eternal rewards. Don't you?

The *"you"* Peter was addressing in 1 Peter 5:4 are the pastors: *"and when the Chief Shepherd appears, you will receive a crown of glory that does not fade away."* There is a crown in heaven for pastors only! The Lord Jesus Christ will present this crown when He appears.

> *For the Lord Himself will descend from heaven with a shout, with the voice of an archangel, and with the trumpet of God. And the dead in Christ will rise first. Then we who are alive and remain shall be caught up together with them in the clouds to meet the Lord in the air. And thus we shall always be with the Lord* (1 Thessalonians 4:16-17).

Jesus will appear at the rapture, our resurrection, as described in 1 Thessalonians 4:16-17. At that grand and glorious moment, the Owner is going to claim His sheep for eternity. At this time, He will also reward the pastors who have been faithful to feed His flock throughout the church age.

The qualifications for the pastor's crown are outlined in the previous verses of scripture: *"feed the flock of God... taking the oversight,"* do these things *"willingly,"* not for *"filthy lucre"* [dishonest gain] and don't be a dictator but being *"examples to the flock"* (1 Peter 5:2-4 KJV).

The office of the pastor is unique because it is a type of the Lord Jesus Christ. As He is Head over the universal Church, the pastor is head over the local church. The pastor should reflect Jesus' character and leadership, leading, feeding, and loving his flock as Jesus does the body of Christ.

The office of the pastor is also unique within the five offices—apostles, prophets, evangelists, pastors, and teachers—because only the pastor is called to stay with one local body of believers. The other ministry gifts travel and are called to all believers. It doesn't mean a pastor cannot travel from time to time, but his highest duties and obligations are within the local church.

In the book of Revelation, Jesus refers to the pastors as stars He holds in His right hand, which represents strength. No two stars in the heavens are exactly the same. Just as God gives each pastor a unique vision, no two churches are exactly the same. The stars that we observe in our universe vary in size and brightness, but every star shines. Just as stars are limited in their brilliance, no one church will reach the entire world. Each church has their unique part to play, but the moment a church says that it will encompass the whole earth, it has stepped into the shoes of Jesus Himself. He is the Sun, and He is the One who will light the whole world!

Each church should be the size and brilliance God has called it to be. Be thankful for the privilege of bringing the gospel to the people and making disciples for the kingdom. It should not be envious or jealous of what another church has or is doing, nor should it try to imitate others. The best thing any pastor, minister, ministry, or church can do is to be themselves and imitate Jesus. Our eyes should be fixed on Him!

As a pastor, people pat you on the back and give you many things. I have plaques, awards, diplomas, and ordination papers all over my wall. I have certificates from organizations that I highly respect. These things are wonderful and I'm grateful for them, but they will one day fade away.

The greatest rewards will come when I stand before Jesus. And the rewards I receive from Him will never fade away (1 Peter 1:4)!

Chapter 11

GOD GIVES GRACE TO THE HUMBLE

Likewise you younger people, submit yourselves to your elders. Yes, all of you be submissive to one another, and be clothed with humility, for "God resists the proud, But gives grace to the humble." Therefore, humble yourselves under the mighty hand of God, that He may exalt you in due time (1 Peter 5:5-6).

In these verses of scripture from 1 Peter 5, Peter has changed his focus from the responsibilities of the pastor to the responsibilities of the congregation. The Bible gives us a clear picture of the structure of the local church, how people flow with the pastor, and how individual believers should relate to one another.

Peter began, *"Likewise you younger people submit yourselves to your elders...."* Literally, this means, "Likewise, you immature, submit yourselves to the mature." Peter was instructing the congregation to submit to their pastor in spiritual matters.

This does not necessarily mean the pastor is more intelligent than anybody else; there will always be people in the congregation who are more highly educated and intelligent than the pastor. However, it does mean that pastors should stay at least one step ahead of everybody with respect to the Word of God.

Some pastors read these verses and wrongly conclude they are supposed to know everything about everything. But that is impossible. You can't know everything! No one can. If I needed help with something on the practical or natural side of running the church, I would draw someone in from the congregation who had expertise in that area, who could assist me or my staff in what we were trying to accomplish.

For example, when it comes to computers, all I know wouldn't fill a teaspoon! So, I get help from someone who knows computers, and I submit to him in that area.

A pastor's calling demands only that he be mature in the Word of God and the moving of the Holy Spirit. And as he is faithful in that area, the congregation can confidently submit to him in spiritual matters.

BE CLOTHED WITH HUMILITY

First Peter 5:5 goes on to say, "*Yes, all of you be submissive to one another, and be clothed with humility....*" The Kenneth

Wuest translation says, *"Moreover, all of you, clothe your-selves with humility toward one another...."*

Many Christians believe "humility" means to be low, downtrodden, and even poor. Humility actually means lowliness of mind, which is an attitude. This attitude is best described in Romans 12:3 where we are exhorted not to think of ourselves more highly than we ought to think. The key to having a servant's heart and a teachable attitude, is to clothe ourselves with humility, to cultivate a submissive attitude at all times and in all situations.

When believers adopt a submissive attitude toward others, whether they are dealing with their boss or their children, they become servants to all people. Those in submission don't think of themselves as being less important or more important than any other human being. They are powerfully aware God considers every person valuable, unique, and special. The opposite of a submissive attitude is pride.

The quickest way for believers to stop receiving the Word of God and growing spiritually is to get puffed up with arrogance and pride, or to think of themselves as spiritually superior to their pastor and to the rest of the congregation. Prideful people are so busy picking apart everything the pastor says, they are unable to receive anything from God through him.

Being *"clothed with humility"* is the believer's responsibility. Like faithfulness and commitment, the pastor can preach and teach it, but in the end the believer must choose to do it. This is self-discipline. God established the local church to help believers become disciples—disciplined to the Word of God.

When a person is born again, he automatically becomes a believer and a member of the universal Church. But to become a disciple, he must submit himself to instruction in a local church. Jesus did not tell us to go into all the world and make "converts" of all nations. He said to make *"disciples"* of all nations (Matthew 28:19-20). The main purpose of the local church is to turn converts into disciples (Ephesians 4:12).

The new birth delivers us out of Satan's kingdom, sin, and from spiritual death. Discipleship gets the sin out of us. Being a disciple will cause our minds to be renewed with the Word of God. This, in turn, results in our sanctification, so that through Him we can overcome sin in our everyday lives. We begin to see and approach life through the mind of Christ.

Often it is said God delivered the children of Israel out of Egypt, but He never got Egypt out of the children of Israel. Many Christians today will not submit or discipline themselves to learn from a pastor of a local church. God has delivered them from the world, but has never got the world out of them!

When a believer does not submit to a pastor and become involved in a local church, it is because of pride. This prideful attitude will usually keep him from walking in humility toward other believers as well. Because submitting to a pastor seems beneath him, other believers who do so will also seem beneath him. Therefore, he cannot walk in an attitude of humility toward other believers either.

The reason the believers never grow up in God is found in the last part of 1 Peter 5:5, *"...God resists the proud, but gives grace to the humble."* You need the grace of God to live the Christian life and to grow up spiritually. God only pours out His grace on *"the humble"*—those who have a submissive attitude.

The humble believer knows he needs God's grace to do all God has called him to do. But the proud person believes not only can he do everything himself, but he can also do it better than anyone else.

The difference between the proud believer and the humble believer can be found in verse 6, which says, *"Humble yourselves under the mighty hand of God...."* In scripture, the hand of God is always a symbol of the supernatural. It is the height of arrogance to think you can do what only the hand of God can do. Therefore, according to this verse, His hand also represents a hand of grace.

To the believer, God's hand is an open hand, filled with all of His provision, wisdom, and strength. The humble man gladly reaches out and receives the supernatural grace of God that is extended to him. He knows he cannot succeed in the Christian life without it. He also knows no believer deserves it, but can receive it through faith in the Word of God.

The proud believer pictures the hand of God as being a closed fist. He must rely on himself to get through life. And because he sees only a closed fist, he rejects the supernatural leadership of the pastor and the fellowship of other believers, who are all part of the open hand of God.

No pastor knows everything about the Word of God, and there is no perfect local church. The Holy Spirit will move on the pastor to speak whatever his people need for the moment. God will even lead one believer to minister to another believer.

But if a believer will not *"be clothed with humility,"* if he will not submit to the pastor or receive from other believers, he will miss what God wants to minister to his life.

After a Christian humbles himself under God's hand and receives from those God is using to speak to him, he must next obey. In this manner, he is now prepared not only to hear from God, but also to be used by God to minister to others.

THE POWER OF SUBMISSION

Submission is an act of our will. We are to *"clothe"* ourselves with humility toward others. Our responsibility is to humble ourselves. God's responsibility is to exalt us in due season.

All believers are priests before our great High Priest, and ultimately answer to Jesus. In other words, in eternal terms, we are always to be in submission to the Lord Jesus Christ.

However, there are times when God commands us to submit to other people—bosses, parents, teachers—believers and unbelievers alike. Whether we like our boss or not, submission is good for us. During those times we are under submission, we learn how to better handle authority.

For example, if a police officer is directing traffic at the intersection you are passing through, for the time that you are in that intersection, you must submit to the police officer's authority. When you are at work, you submit to your boss; but when you are at home, you are the boss. Submitting to someone you don't like or agree with helps to make you a more compassionate boss.

Submission is relative. Who you submit to depends on where you are at the moment. And no matter who you are or where you are, you are always in the sandwich of authority. Someone may be under you, but someone is always above you. God sits at the top. The music minister is the head of worship, but he is still submitted to the pastor; the husband is head of the family, but Christ is the Head of the man (1 Corinthians 11:3).

No believer is an island unto himself or his own boss, because each of us will ultimately answer to Jesus. When we submit ourselves to a pastor and commit ourselves to a local church, we are submitting ourselves to God, to His Word, and to His Spirit. There is no limit to the miracles God can do in our lives when we discipline and commit ourselves in this manner!

Jesus marveled at the faith of the centurion because of his simple understanding of authority: *"For I also am a man under authority, having soldiers under me…"* (Matthew 8:9). Because he understood the power of submission to authority, the centurion received a great and mighty miracle!

AUTHORITY AND SUBMISSION

The whole earth operates under a system of authority and submission, which serves to hold the world together and causes us to live in peace despite the devil's operation. Without levels of authority, chaos and confusion would reign in our lives.

The more you understand authority and submission, the more you can grow in God, because *"God gives grace to the humble."* If you persist in rebelling against authority, in harboring an unsubmissive attitude, you are rebelling against God, the Source of all authority.

Authority and submission will only work among equals. Without equality, you only have slavery; but where equality is stressed, submission is no problem.

For example, when the husband considers his wife to be his equal and treats her accordingly, she has no problem submitting to him. Likewise, when the wife understands she is equal with her husband, she can joyfully submit to his authority and there is peace in the home.

In Romans 8:17, we are called *"joint heirs with Christ."* We are seated with Him in heaven (see Ephesians 2:6). The work of the cross has made us equal in position to Christ. Therefore, submission to Him comes naturally. There is equality in worth, but hierarchy in function.

Throughout the Word of God, there are references to levels of authority in the local church. The mere mention of *"bishop, overseer, elder, pastor"* indicate God has set a hierarchy of responsibility in our churches to establish order and keep the peace.

A pastor, elder, bishop, or deacon is no better than anyone else in the congregation. If they believe they are, they are headed for a fall. If the pastor stresses equality in the church, submission will have little resistance. The term "pastor" must mean there is a congregation. "Shepherd" means there are sheep. "Leader" means there are followers, and "authority" means submission must follow.

There is no way around this fact—your pastor is *"over you in the Lord"* (1 Thessalonians 5:12). This verse does not say your pastor is over you in your natural life; he is over you in your spiritual life.

Over the years there has been some distortion of the doctrine of submission and authority in the local church. In fact, today you can mention submission to some believers, and they will close their ears and turn away in disgust or fear. This is because the doctrine of submission and authority was taken to an extreme. Because the pastor believed himself to be superior, submission meant slavery.

In extreme teachings on submission the pastor or designated elder exercises authority over both natural and spiritual areas of their congregational members' lives. Believers in these churches are expected to get approval from an elder or the pastor for every decision they make. This can range from which car to buy to which person they should marry.

But the pastor's responsibility is not to control. His responsibility is to "lead and feed," to pray and carry out the vision for that local church and to preach and teach the Word of God to the believers God has entrusted to his care. The pastor and staff of elders, the bishops and deacons who serve him, are in authority *"over"* the congregation in spiritual areas only.

Just from a practical standpoint, living the Word of God is a twenty-four-hour-a-day job for everyone! Trying to follow everyone in your congregation around to make sure they are living it too, would be impossible!

If a member of the congregation is having difficulty making a decision in certain areas, godly counsel and advice in line with the Word of God should be made available. However, the pastor or a staff member should be giving counsel, not making demands.

Your job as pastor is to *"admonish"* the people or put them in remembrance of God's Word (1 Thessalonians 5:12). You are not to dictate to them. A dictator's view of authority and submission removes equality from the system. And without equality, submission and authority become a system of slavery. Because of this viewpoint of authority and submission, some believers have ignored this scriptural doctrine and have gone to the other extreme, which is rebellion.

These believers, in their hurt and disillusionment, choose to wander from church to church, refusing to submit to the leadership of a pastor. They have a resentful attitude toward all authority, assuming any authority is corrupt. As a result, they cannot grow in God, and they become even more frustrated and bitter.

Others, after being pressured into ungodly submission by one pastor, find it difficult to even trust God to lead them to another church where they can freely submit and commit themselves. They are brokenhearted and need to be healed.

That healing will come as they ask God to show them which local body of believers is their church home, submit themselves to a pastor, and "put their hand to the plow" to work. If they will do this, not only will they begin to grow again spiritually, but they will also place themselves in a position to be mightily blessed of God. If we humble ourselves under the mighty hand of God, He will exalt us.

THE ENEMY OF HUMILITY

Pride, which is the enemy of humility, is the opposite of a submissive attitude. Pride occurs when you elevate your-self above someone else for any reason. If Satan can cause a pastor or a congregation to enter into pride—thinking themselves to be better than others—he can destroy the body of believers.

Believers can view themselves as better than others in both spiritual and natural areas. Spiritual pride is bigotry. Natural pride is prejudice.

Bigotry is intolerance toward other believers who do not believe what you believe about a certain area of the Word of God. For example, many churches today do not believe in speaking with tongues. They interpret the scriptures on tongues different from those who do speak with tongues.

You can find spiritual bigots on both sides of this issue. There are those who will not associate with a believer if he speaks with tongues, but there are also those who will not associate with any believer who does not. They are both spiritual bigots because they elevate themselves above other Christians who think differently than they do.

It is very important to understand when a believer is a spiritual bigot, it is because of his attitude, not because of the issue about which he is intolerant. Some churches speak with tongues and walk in love toward churches that don't. Some churches don't speak with tongues but walk in love toward churches that do!

The Bible says, *"endeavoring to keep the unity of the Spirit in the bond of peace"* (Ephesians 4:3). Vision unites a church, not doctrine. Only our simple faith in Jesus Christ as the Lord and Savior of our lives, our common love for Him, and the desire to win souls will bring the body of believers together and cause one local church to walk in love with another local church.

Even with each local church, you will find many different opinions about the more controversial doctrines, like end-time prophecy. Satan will try to incite spiritual bigotry over these issues with the purpose of dividing the church.

But none of these issues affect our eternal salvation or the fulfilling of the great commission. Doctrinal differences cannot affect the unity of the church when we understand this and choose to have a love and respect for each believer while maintaining a submissive attitude.

Prejudice involves pride toward natural areas in life. One of the most subtle tactics of the devil bringing division is prejudice toward other believers because of a natural attribute, such as race, color, sex, or social status.

Galatians 3:28 says, *"There is neither Jew nor Greek, there is neither slave nor free, there is neither male nor female; for you are all one in Christ Jesus."* Whatever is true for the universal Church is also true for the local church.

In the universal Church, God does not recognize race, social class, or gender. Therefore, in the local church, neither should we place any significance on these things. When God looks at the universal Church, He sees us as one body; when we look at our local church, we too should see ourselves as one body.

In Ephesians 2:11 we are told before we were born again, we were *"Gentiles in the flesh."* In other words, race and skin color only exist in the flesh, not in the spirit. God doesn't see us according to nationalities. In fact, in heaven He won't put the Jews in one corner and the Gentiles in another. All believers are one in the body of Christ.

Galatians 3:28 says that *"there is neither bond nor free."* In other words, there are no social distinctions in the body of Christ. God doesn't favor the rich over the poor; nor does He favor the poor over the rich (James 2:1-9).

One of my favorite illustrations of our equality in Christ is found in the Old Testament when David danced before the Lord (2 Samuel 6:16). Michal, David's wife, looked out her window and saw *"King David leaping and whirling before the Lord; and she despised him in her heart."*

Michal did not despise David merely for making a public spectacle of himself. She despised him because he had removed his kingly robes and was parading himself as a common priest. All he wore was his priestly ephod. She looked down on David with prideful eyes because he had humbled himself before his people and made a statement by his actions that in God there is no class hierarchy—no bond or free.

Michal's security and identity were in natural things rather than spiritual truths. She had loved David because he was the king, not because he was a child of God. She valued him only for his position.

This should not be so in the church. When we walk into the local church, we should be more aware than ever that beneath our lawyer's suit, our welder's clothes, our nurse's uniform, is merely a blood-bought member of the body of Christ. We need to remove all facades and be who we really are—equal in the sight of God.

It is a blessing to watch people from every background praising and worshipping God together as one body. A garbage collector turns to give a word of encouragement to a doctor. An engineer prays for a waitress to be healed, while a young college student joins hands with an elderly woman to agree for her needs to be met.

Galatians 3:28 says that in Christ *"there is neither male nor female."* God makes no distinction between male and female in the Church.

In natural matters, if a woman is married, she is submissive to her husband. But where spiritual matters are concerned, she is under the headship of Jesus Christ. Church history confirms God moves as mightily through women as He does through men. Joel prophesied that sons and daughters, servants and handmaidens would prophesy (Acts 2:17-18 KJV).

Although men and women are both equal in Christ, they are each better suited for particular natural functions in the local church. Deacons and elders can be either male or female, yet I didn't have female ushers in our church. Ushers may be called on to help handicapped people out of cars, restrain the unruly, carry in chairs or move the pulpit, and men are better suited physically for these jobs.

Women are wonderfully suited to teaching and ministering to children. They exercise much more patience and care for them than many men would. We have equality in worth, but differences in function.

More men are called into full-time ministry than women. Is God prejudiced? No, that would be blasphemous! God knows the physical limitations of women and calls them into more supportive roles. Some women are called into full-time ministry, but this is the exception and not the rule. The number of men called into full-time ministry found in the Bible, far outnumbers the women called into public ministries.

Jesus Himself had no women disciples, most likely because He knew of the hardships and dangers He would face in His travels. However, women were a major financial support of His ministry (Luke 9:2-3). When all of the disciples forsook Him at His arrest and crucifixion, the women remained with Him (Luke 23:49,55), and they also told the disciples of His resurrection (Luke 24:8-10).

I personally believe the office of the pastor is primarily for men. I know women stand in that office and do an excellent job. They are obviously chosen by God. But the vast number of pastors in the Bible and in society today are men.

The pastor is head of the local body of believers, just as Jesus is the Head of the body of Christ, and the husband is the head of a family. The Bible likens the relationship between the pastor and his congregation to a marriage. Unlike the other ministry offices, the pastor is "married" to his congregation.

One issue I will mention here too, is often in the local church you will find that certain age groups can be neglected, usually children and senior citizens. They are treated as "second-class citizens" of the body of Christ. We always need to remember the older saints have the wisdom of living to impart to us, and the younger saints are the spiritual leaders of tomorrow!

Within every children's church are the future fivefold ministry gifts and the elders, bishops, and deacons of your church for the next generation. There should be just as much concern for their spiritual welfare as for the adults.

In all of these areas—race, social class, gender, and age—the pastor will set the example for the congregation, and then it is up to the congregation to follow. There is nothing more disturbing and disheartening than a pastor who favors one race over another, one social class over another, one gender over another or who is ignoring the needs of different age groups.

When the pastor walks in a submissive attitude, with love toward all men and women, and the congregation follows him, a spirit of love and unity holds the church together so tightly Satan finds no entrance. In this atmosphere of love, faith supernaturally explodes! The church becomes a powerful tool for God in the earth.

THE GLORIOUS CHURCH

The scriptures repeatedly remind us that the natural differences we are confronted with on earth are temporary. They will perish as we rise to meet Jesus in the air (1 Thessalonians 4:16-17). However, while we are in this flesh, we must deal with those differences according to the Word of God.

This means we are to have submissive hearts and attitudes. Whether our boss asks us to perform a task we love or something we dislike, we are to cheerfully obey. Yet if we are asked to do something contrary to the Word of God, we maintain a submissive attitude, but we obey God rather than men.

Let's illustrate by using the husband and wife as an example. The wife is equal to the husband in Christ, but her gender places her in submission to her husband. However, if a husband asks his wife to stop attending church, he is violating the Word of God. Submissively, the wife can refuse to obey. In this way, she obeys God rather than man, yet maintains a submissive attitude.

A submissive attitude brings glory to the Lord Jesus Christ and to His Church.

In 1 Peter 2:9-10 we are told that the Church is *"a chosen generation, a royal priesthood, a holy nation, His own special people…who once* [before we were born again] *were not a people but are now the people of God…."*

This scripture passage in 1 Peter 2 declares the body of Christ is a completely different nation, a God-made race of people, who are unique in every aspect of their lives. They live for God and love one another as He loves them.

Our purpose is to do God's will on earth. In other words, using a military term, we are called to "occupy" until Jesus, our Leader, returns. Contrary to the world's way of thinking, the way the Church "occupies" is to serve. In the kingdom of God, the greatest ruler is the greatest servant.

As the family of God, we are exhorted to clothe ourselves with humility toward one another, to submit ourselves to those in authority over us, and to humble ourselves under the mighty hand of God. According to the Bible, submission is not a place of weakness—it is a place of power.

First Peter 5:6 says, *"Therefore humble yourselves under the mighty hand of God, that He may exalt you in due time."* The phrase *"in due time"* means He will exalt us at just the right moment during our lifetime on earth. We know that time will come in this life, because time will not exist in heaven!

God has an appointed time for the harvest of success and fulfillment for every seed of humility we have sown. The degree to which we are exalted is proportionate to the degree to which we are submissive.

The level of our commitment to serve others will determine the level of His grace, mercy, and power that operates in our lives.

When the local body of believers and their pastor begin to walk in "humility of mind," the supernatural unity that is produced gives them the ability to reach their area for Jesus Christ. They become like one of those brightly lit lampstands of Revelation 1:20, and Jesus is powerfully walking in their midst!

Chapter 12

HOW TO KNOW YOUR PASTOR

And we urge you, brethren, to recognize those who labor among you, and are over you in the Lord and admonish you, and to esteem them very highly in love for their work's sake. Be at peace among yourselves (1 Thessalonians 5:12-13).

The first part of 1 Thessalonians 5:12 says to *"recognize those who labor among you."* It is important for the congregation to know the character and beliefs of their pastor.

You might say, "Well, my church is very large, so how can the pastor possibly let everyone get to know him?" The Greek word for "recognize" in this verse means "to know about" or "to know by observation." It does not indicate an intimate friendship, but a knowledge you acquire of someone as you watch the person from a distance.

Whenever you hear your pastor preach and teach, you are hearing his heart, you are discovering how he thinks and what he believes. And if you want to know what he expects of you, listen to what he says every time the church doors open, and you will find out!

Nobody can have more than a few close friends, especially when you are married and have a family, and the pastor is no exception. You can't expect your pastor to be every member's best friend, but you can get to know him as you listen to his sermons and observe how he handles the challenges of his own life.

PASTORS ARE HUMAN

Sometimes church members who don't have a close personal relationship with the pastor tend to believe he is superhuman—that he doesn't have to deal with the same problems they face every day. This is why I exhort pastors to be themselves in the pulpit, to let their people see them "at all seasons" (Chapter 2).

What many believers don't realize is God calls regular human beings into the ministry, and they are full of mistakes, failures, troubles, and trials just like anybody else.

One time someone approached me and said, "You don't deserve to be in the pulpit." I agreed. Then I reminded them that they didn't deserve to be in the congregation either. All of us are where we are because of the grace of God, and we need to understand this and remind ourselves of it as we submit to those in authority and as we submit to one another.

I have learned even the most spiritual among us are human. I have learned when a spiritual leader makes a mistake, the believers who follow him make a choice—they will either judge the leader and forsake him or extend grace to the leader as Jesus extends grace to them when they fail.

I'm not talking about sin, and especially persistent sin. If the pastor or a spiritual leader is involved in something immoral or illegal, discipline must follow. But what I'm referring to are errors in judgment that every believer makes in their daily walk with the Lord.

The reason 1 Thessalonians 5:13 says the congregation should *"esteem them* [pastors] *very highly in love for their work's sake,"* is because the pastor is to be esteemed for the position in which God has placed him. In other words, you esteem and love your pastor for the office he stands in, for his preaching and teaching the Word of God, not because he is perfect.

PASTORS LABOR AND ADMONISH

Some church members think the pastor's job consists of preaching a few sermons a week, counseling a few people, and playing golf the rest of the time. The ministry is work, and the pressures that go with it can be intense.

That is one of the reasons I have written this book! I believe I can help other pastors enjoy their calling and increase their effectiveness because God has taught me how to do this in my own ministry. I enjoy praying and studying the Word of God. I love preaching and teaching under the Spirit's power and seeing people transformed as they receive from God. Sometimes I am astounded I get paid for what I love to do!

The problems and the pressures come with people. There are times I could not understand *why* some people reacted the way they did and thought what they thought! But my job was to love them anyway, to continue to lead them and feed them with the Word of God.

This is where the *"admonishing"* part of the pastor enters into the picture. In Hebrews 10:24 the Holy Spirit tells us to *"consider one another in order to stir up love and good works."*

As a pastor, you are called to admonish the people, which means to put them in remembrance of God's Word. And sometimes this means you must *"stir up"* the sheep to *"love and good works."* The phrase "stir up" means to push toward a destination. Sometimes this is not a pleasant experience!

When the congregation isn't walking in love or good works in some area, the Holy Spirit will help you provoke them with His Word. If it doesn't work the first time, He will have you do it again.

The pastor is not the only one who does the provoking. Hebrews 10:25 goes on to say, *"Not forsaking the assembling of ourselves together...but exhorting one another...."* The congregation has a responsibility toward each other too. If someone in the church sees another member falter in their life of faith or get off into error, the

Holy Spirit will often lead them to *"stir up"* their friend back to walking in love and good works.

For example, if someone you know in the church becomes offended and begins to harbor a grudge, God may call upon you to humbly remind your friend that in order to continue walking *"in love and good works,"* they must forgive the person who has offended them and give the situation to the Lord.

This doesn't give us a license to go around slapping each other with the Word of God! These verses actually teach us about our true responsibility toward one another. By provoking each other, we eliminate pride. You cannot go to a brother or sister and *stir up love and good works* if you go to them in arrogance, nor can you stir up love and good works by someone unless you have a submissive attitude.

Once the pastor gives the congregation God's Word on the subject, once he stirs up the congregation to love and good works, it is then up to the congregation to put that Word into effect in their lives as they live, work, and minister together.

The purpose of the pastor is found in Ephesians 4:12, *"For the equipping of the saints for the work of the ministry, for the edifying of the body of Christ."* The primary function of the pastor is to feed the sheep—to preach and teach the Word of God.

The fivefold ministry gifts listed in Ephesians 4:11 are called to perfect the saints for the work of the ministry.

It is the congregation who goes out into the world to be a witness, to preach the gospel to their neighbors and coworkers, to pray for the sick, to bring the Word of God to the streets of their city.

The work of the ministry is not confined to the four walls of the local church, it extends to the highways and byways through the congregation. I would admonish my people to take the Word of God that is spoken from the pulpit and apply it to their lives. Resist temptation. Raise up a godly family in a God-rejecting world. Be the best worker in their company. Take their offenses and complaints to the Lord and handle them according to His will. Be a living testimony to the world of the power of the gospel of Jesus Christ.

The pastor can admonish, but he cannot force the congregation to go out and live the Word. Sometimes the Holy Spirit would lead me in a particular direction during the sermon, and I would know with a certainty that one or more of the members of the church were failing in that area.

There are also times when the Holy Spirit would lead me off into an area and I would visibly see people squirming in their seats. However, I would assure my church that although the Holy Spirit may tell me *what* to say—He never tells me *who* I'm talking about! One of the greatest gifts God has given us in the body of Christ is *privacy!*

The Holy Spirit will convict the sinning believer through the Word He leads the pastor to preach, but He will *never* publicly humiliate someone from the pulpit. I never knew what was going on in the private lives of the members of our church unless they told me.

I will never forget an incident that occurred while I was teaching from the book of Proverbs. The Holy Spirit had led me to describe the difference between the *"strange woman"* (the prostitute) and the *"evil woman"* (the adulteress). The Bible teaches the prostitute is only after a man's money, but the adulteress wants to possess his entire life!

As the service closed, a woman came running down the aisle, pointed her finger in my face, and cried, "I'm not after his life! Who talked to you?" Of course no one had ever spoken to me about her. I would have never known anything if she had remained silent. An old proverb says, "When you throw a rock into a pack of dogs, the one who is hit yells."

Personally, I would rather not have known the intimate details of the congregation's lives. I didn't want my sermons or my ministry to the people to be tainted because I knew certain things about them. When I pray for someone to be healed, I wouldn't want to be thinking, "Well, they only gave a small offering last week, and I know that a tenth of their salary is much greater. They don't deserve to be healed!"

I wouldn't want to be tempted to avoid certain subjects the Holy Spirit is urging me to teach from the Word of God because of concern that someone in the congregation involved in sin or error may be offended. Neither would I want my flesh to pressure me to emphasize something because I knew someone was sinning in an area.

The less the pastor knows about the private lives of his congregation, the easier it is for him to minister in the freedom of the Holy Spirit. If necessary and if possible, the counseling and visitation workers should minister to the people on a more intimate level.

ON A PEDESTAL

First Thessalonians 5:13 exhorts members of the congregation to *"esteem them* [pastors] *very highly in love for their work's sake."* The word "esteem" means to consider, and this verse says to *"consider them very highly."* In other words, the people should put their pastor on a pedestal.

The word "works" refers to everything the pastor gives the congregation and the fruit produced through his ministry. The pastor is to be put on a pedestal and to be loved by his people because of the work—the production he does on their behalf.

This verse is saying the pastor should be honored because of what he does and because he stands in the office of a pastor, *not* because of his personality. If he tells great jokes, is very friendly, and loves dogs and children, that is wonderful. But if he is quiet, keeps to himself, and chooses to remain single, you should still respect him and submit to him for the spiritual guidance and teaching he brings.

When I first took the church I pastored, I owned a Pontiac Trans Am. One of the members of the congregation told me they didn't think a pastor should drive this kind of car—that it would offend people. Their solution was for me to buy a more "acceptable" automobile.

My response was, "I've found that no car manufacturer makes 'pastor's cars,' and I like this one. It meets my needs." Because I would not exchange my car for the kind of car they thought I should drive, they left the church.

Can you imagine that individual standing before Jesus and Jesus asking, "Why did you leave the church I called you to?" The person would have to reply, "Because the pastor drove a Trans Am!"

This may sound trivial, but unfortunately this sort of thing happens in churches much more than you might think! People will get born again in church, their lives will be changed, their families restored, and one day they are offended and leave the church because the pastor has made a decision or set a policy that does not agree with them. The new building has chairs instead of pews, the new carpet is blue instead of tan, or the pastor bought a more expensive house than they have.

When people submit to the leadership of a pastor and commit themselves to a local body of believers, eventually something will happen to cause them to be offended or disappointed. As they get to know their pastor better, they will have to go through the process of having him fall off the pedestal as his faults, weaknesses, and personality become known, and then putting him back up there by the Word and God's grace!

I can almost guarantee that the devil will make sure that whatever things hurt or offend them will be done to them by someone in the church, usually by someone they would least expect, and possibly even by the pastor himself.

If believers don't handle the offense according to the Word of God, then everything they see will be colored by their hurt or anger. Suddenly the pastor doesn't seem to be anointed anymore. Close friends in the congregation are excited about the sermon or coming events in the church, but those who have been offended will have a negative attitude. If not dealt with, the offense will grow to the degree that nothing satisfies them.

Until they ask God to forgive them and rid themselves of bitterness and resentment, the offended will be miserable. Basically, their pride is separating them from fellowship with God and their brothers and sisters in Christ.

There will also be decisions and policies coming down from leadership that will displease people. When they make their opinion known, those in authority may not see it their way in the end. These are not valid reasons for leaving a church.

Believers may leave a church because the leadership has been engaging in habitual and unrepented sin or heretical teaching of the Word of God—not because the pastor's wife sings the solo every Sunday or the offering is collected in buckets instead of brass plates!

Believers who storm out of the church because of an offense or a difference of opinion should ask themselves these important questions:

- Is the pastor preaching and teaching the Word of God?
- Are people being born again, filled with the Spirit, and restored to fellowship with the Lord?
- Is the congregation prospering and growing in the things of God?
- Are families being strengthened?
- And most important, is this where God wants me to be?

These are the important issues in the local church. When the congregation esteems the pastor and church leadership *"for their work's sake,"* 1 Thessalonians 5:13 says they will *"be at peace"* among themselves.

THE BOND OF PEACE

When a pastor and his congregation live in peace, there is no way Satan can get his foot in the door, and there is no limit to what God can do. But peace is not something that just drops out of heaven for no reason. Peace is something you battle to maintain.

The greatest leaders of nations will tell you in order to live in peace, they must maintain a strong military defense. Sometimes in order to stay free and keep peace, there is a battle. In Ephesians 4:1-3, Paul exhorts us:

> *I, therefore, the prisoner of the Lord, beseech you to walk worthy of the calling with which you were called, with all lowliness and gentleness, with longsuffering, bearing with one another in love, endeavoring to keep the unity of the Spirit in the bond of peace.*

We are unified spiritually because we are born again, but Paul is urging us to allow this spiritual unity to extend into the natural realm—where we live with one another. We wage this battle to maintain peace in our lives and in our churches. The essence of unity manifests when we walk in love toward one another.

Walking in unity with God is not as difficult as walking in unity with each other. Ephesians 4:3 says walking in unity with each other is an *"endeavor."* In other words, it is work! I know God loves me, and I know I can count on Him, but I'm not so sure about other people!

That's why many Christians stay home and watch Christian television instead of going to church and getting involved. The difficult part of the Christian life is rubbing shoulders with other believers, each with their own set of problems, and submitting to a pastor who is less than perfect.

"How can I praise the Lord when the sister sitting next to me is singing so loudly in my ear? Every time we have praise and worship, she is so off-key; she gives a whole new meaning to making a joyful noise! And I just know that Brother Bill will sit next to me and ask me to join the ushers again. And I really wish that a certain family would discipline their children—honestly, they are trashing the Sunday school rooms!"

In previous scripture verses cited, Paul describes the battle to keep the *"unity of the Spirit"* as walking *"worthy of the calling with which you are called* [being faithful on the job], *with all lowliness* [humility, a submissive attitude] *and gentleness* [a teachable heart], *with longsuffering* [patience], *bearing with* [putting up with] *one another in love."*

It takes effort to walk in love, but the result is living in peace and unity in the body of Christ. Unity is one of the special blessings that comes with being a member of God's family. Only believers can enjoy the *"unity of the Spirit"* that comes from walking in love, because the Bible says that the *"love of God has been poured out in our hearts by the Holy Spirit who was given to us"* (Romans 5:5).

The world can come together against a common enemy or for a common cause. They can sign a temporary truce in war, but they will never have peace or unity; peace and unity is a result of walking in love toward one another and comes from the Holy Spirit.

Most importantly, there is a supernatural power that accompanies the *"unity of the Spirit."* In Matthew 18:19-20, Jesus says, *"...if two of you agree on earth concerning anything that they ask, it will be done for them by My Father in heaven. For where two or three are gathered together in My name, I am there in the midst of them."* Jesus, the High Priest of the Church, walks in the midst of us when we agree. When we are in agreement, the miracle-working power of God is released!

Jesus is not commanding us to agree about our doctrines; He is telling us to agree in prayer about a need so the need can be met.

Many believers think the ultimate sign of maturity in the Christian life is faith. But faith is only the beginning. The ultimate sign of maturity in the Christian life is love—*agape love* (see 2 Peter 1:5-7). This is the God kind of love. *"But God demonstrates His own love toward us, in that while we were still sinners, Christ died for us"* (Romans 5:8).

Love will put aside personal differences to see someone saved, healed, and set free. Ephesians 4:3 says the unity of the Spirit is kept in the *"bond of peace."* The bond of peace is the believer's commitment to choose to walk in love toward other believers regardless of the challenges raised by the world, the devil, or the flesh.

While you are on this earth, the Church will never walk in the unity of doctrines, traditions, politics, or personal preferences. But you can overcome your differences with others and achieve *"unity of the Spirit in the bond of peace."* When the Holy Spirit is allowed to reign in our lives, *"the love of God is shed abroad in our hearts,"* and you can walk in love toward one another. This is the bond of peace in action.

You can submit to your pastor, love him, *"esteem him highly for his work's sake,"* and still not agree with everything he preaches and teaches. And you can rub shoulders with the most unusual people, pray with them and see God move mountains. How? By *"endeavoring* [choosing to walk in love] *to keep the unity of the Spirit in the bond of peace."*

Because the explosive supernatural power of God is present when a pastor and his congregation live in unity and peace, the Church is constantly being bombarded by Satan's attacks. Satan knows if he can divide us, particularly if he can incite the flesh to rise up in strife and contention, we are powerless. He also knows if we stand together in love, we can take the gospel into all the world.

Unity and peace are established in the local church by the heart of the pastor. The bond of peace—the commitment to walk in love toward others—*must begin with leadership.*

We have discussed how you can know your pastor by his works, and *"esteem him highly for his work's sake,"* which is to labor in the Word of God and prayer and to admonish the people. This is how you know his beliefs. But of equal importance is to know your pastor's character.

You know a person's character by observing the manifestation of the fruit of the Spirit in the person's life.

Galatians 5:22-23 (KJV) names these godly character traits as *"love, joy, peace, longsuffering* [patience], *gentleness, goodness* [purity], *faith* [faithfulness], *meekness* [teachable attitude], and *temperance* [self-control]...."

Jesus said we would know them by their fruit, which is also a reference to the same fruit of the Spirit found in Galatians 5. Luke 6:44-45 says:

> *For every tree is known by its own fruit. For men do not gather figs from thorns, nor do they gather grapes from a bramble bush. A good man out of the good treasure of his heart brings forth good; and an evil man out of the evil treasure of his heart brings forth evil. For out of the abundance of the heart his mouth speaks.*

How can you love, esteem, and submit to your pastor and still have major differences in various areas? The answer is *because you know his character.* You see the fruit of the Spirit in his life, His heart is after God, his desire is to serve God and the people, he loves his congregation and prays for them, he is faithful to study and teach the Word of God and then live it to the best of his ability, and there is a consistent stability and joy in his life because of these things.

Therefore, you know your pastor by listening to his sermons and observing his manner of life. These things reveal his beliefs and his character.

The relationship between a pastor and his congregation is very special. God gives the pastor a love for his people that sees beyond their weaknesses and failures to all they can be in Christ. His every effort is focused on helping them to grow spiritually, encouraging them to know their God more intimately through the Holy Spirit, and giving them the knowledge and wisdom from God's Word to live fulfilled, prosperous lives.

When the congregation knows their pastor is committed to them, that he will walk in love toward them and be a faithful example for them, many will easily accept his leadership, commit themselves to be part of the ministry of the church, and begin to walk in love toward each other.

The Bible says, *"faith working through love"* (Galatians 5:6), and faith is the supernatural power by which mountains are removed and captives set free. The trigger for this vast power is love.

When a pastor chooses to love his congregation in word and deed, and the members respond by following his example, the local church becomes an awesome powerhouse through which God can reach a generation for Jesus Christ.

Like the church at Ephesus, a pastor and congregation who commit themselves to keep the faith and walk in love are empowered to bring the mighty, healing hands of Jesus to the broken and hurting people in their community. It is through great local churches, walking in the demonstration of God's Word and in the power of the Holy Spirit, that God can move mightily in cities, in nations, and throughout the world!

Chapter 13

MANY MEMBERS, ONE BODY

*For as we have many members in one body, but
all the members do not have the same function,
so we, being many, are one body in Christ, and
individually members of one another* (Romans
12:4-5).

PAULS' MESSAGE—THE BODY OF CHRIST

Unity in the local church and in the universal Church
between each believer and the Lord Jesus was important
to Paul and should be important to us. He mentioned
more about unity in the local churches than any other
writer of the New Testament epistles. No other New
Testament writer mentions Jesus as the Head of the
Church or us as His Body. Paul *alone* teaches Christ as the
Head of the Church and believers as the body of Christ.
He *alone* teaches about each Christian being a member
of Christ's body and how the members work together.
Not only is Paul the only one who teaches about the

body of Christ, He speaks about it nine different times in his writings (see Romans 12:4-5; 1 Corinthians 6:15, 12:12-27; Ephesians 1:22-23, 3:6, 4:12,16, 5:23; Colossians 1:18,24, 2:10,19).

WHAT CIRCUMSTANCES LED TO SAUL'S CONVERSION?

To properly understand why Paul taught this subject so intensely, we must go back to the circumstances leading to his conversion on the road to Damascus. The following is the first revelation Paul, then known as Saul, receives, showing him Jesus was the Messiah and His close attachment to everyone who believes in Him:

They [the Jewish leaders] *cast him* [Stephen] *out of the city and stoned him. And the witnesses laid down their clothes at the feet of a young man named Saul. And they stoned Stephen, as he was calling on God and saying, "Lord Jesus, receive my spirit." Then he knelt down and cried out with a loud voice, "Lord, do not charge them with this sin." And when he had said this, he fell asleep.*

Now Saul was consenting to his death.

At that time [Stephen's death] *great persecution arose against the church which was at Jerusalem; and they were all scattered throughout the regions of Judea and Samaria, except the apostles. And devout men carried Stephen to his burial and made great lamentation over him.*

As for Saul, he made havoc of the church, entering every house, and dragging off men and women and committing them to prison. Therefore, those who were scattered went everywhere preaching the word (Acts 7:58-8:4).

The Jewish leaders were dumbfounded at the rise of the Christians like no group had risen before. Individuals had risen before with a few followers but were soon killed and their movements ended. These Christians were dedicated to the crucified Jesus and were growing in numbers daily and rapidly. Persecution from the Jews and Romans only caused them to increase in numbers and fervour.

The Christians were extremely dangerous to the Jews because they taught that man is not saved by keeping the Jewish law and people no longer needed to go to the temple for salvation, forgiveness, or spiritual growth. They also were common people. Many, who were formerly nonreligious, were all moved with the same fervour, dedication, and love for their Lord and each other. They declared their love for each other, and their zeal came from the Lord Jesus, claiming He was the Messiah.

They also had the same power Jesus had to heal the sick, perform miracles, and see people raised from the dead. Even in death, the level of unity in the Christians had never been seen before. This so frightened and incensed the Jewish leaders that they sent Saul out to kill Christians.

Saul was greatly dedicated to the Jewish religion of his fathers. He remained faithful to the only form of religion he had ever known and zealously defended it against this new apostasy. Moses' law declared that anyone who spoke against the Law was to be cut off from Israel, even killed. Such people in the time of Moses were stoned to death and Saul had just consented to and witnessed Stephen's death.

After Stephen's death, because of great Jewish religious opposition, more persecution against Christians broke out in Jerusalem and spread to Gentile cities, headed up by Saul, who later wrote to the Galatian church, *"I advanced in Judaism* [Jewish religion] *beyond many of my contemporaries in my own nation, being more exceedingly zealous for the traditions of my fathers"* (Galatians 1:14).

The next time we read about Saul he was headed for Damascus to kill Christians. Think about that! Damascus is in Syria. Saul was headed toward an Arab city to hunt for Christians, drag them from their houses, imprison them in Jerusalem, and kill them.

> *Then Saul, still breathing threats and murder against the disciples of the Lord, went to the high priest and asked letters from him to the synagogues of Damascus, so that if he found any who were of the Way, whether men or women, he might bring them bound to Jerusalem.*

As he journeyed he came near Damascus, and suddenly a light shone around him from heaven. Then he fell to the ground, and heard a voice saying to him, "Saul, Saul, why are you persecuting Me?" (Acts 9:1-4)

SAUL'S CONVERSION

Saul recognized the voice of Jehovah, but was surprised by what He said, *"Why are you persecuting ME?"* This meant that the Lord he thought he was serving was the One these Christians were serving. This also meant that the Jesus he had been fighting was truly the Messiah he had been waiting for all his life. He had come and gone, and Saul had not seen it.

Questions had to be coming to him faster than he could get out of his head or mouth. Perhaps he was thinking, "But Lord, I'm not persecuting You, I'm helping You. I'm on Your side. I oversaw the killing of a young man, just a helper in a group of Christians."

No doubt the reply had to be strong, "No Saul, you killed ME."

"But his name was Stephen."

"No, his name was JESUS. *Whatever you do to the least of my brethren, you do to Me.*"

The revelation hit Saul so hard it stayed with him all the way to his death as Paul, Christ's apostle. Christians are united even to death—they are united to each other and equally united to their Savior, Jesus the Messiah. All are one.

JESUS' PRAYER IN THE GARDEN

That they all may be one; as You, Father, are in Me, and I in You; that they also may be one in Us. And the glory which You gave Me I have given them, that they may be one, just as We are one: I in them and You in Me… (John 17:21-23).

I call this the "divine entanglement." I am in the Father because I am in the Son and the Son is in the Father. No one can tell where my life ends, and Jesus' begins. Nor can they tell where Jesus' life ends, and the Father's begins. My life has been totally mingled with the life of Jesus and the life of the Father. Like a blood covenant, where the blood of two individuals is mingled together, I cannot be separated from the Father, the Son, or all other believers. Once mixed, how do you unmingle blood?

At salvation we become Christ. He and we are the whole man. We are as inseparable from Him as He is from the Father. We are one with Him as He is one with the Father.

We can now begin to finally understand the profound meaning of scriptures concerning the body of Christ.

When one member suffers or rejoices, we all suffer and rejoice. To persecute you is to persecute me. To persecute us is to persecute Christ. No wonder I don't have to defend myself when I am persecuted because of my stand as being a Christian. He defends me because He can defend Himself. *"...Vengeance is Mine, I will repay, says the Lord"* (Romans 12:19). When someone breaks your arm, they have struck *you.* Jesus' defense of Stephen caused His meeting with Saul.

Saints from the Day of Pentecost until today form one great body of believers, the body of Christ. We are all part of Jesus, making up His spiritual body on earth. God has willed that the risen Jesus Christ and all believers since that day are to be the body of one Man, the Head, Christ.

THE CRUCIFIXION SEEMS TO BE THE MAIN MESSAGE OF ALL FOUR GOSPELS

Jesus' death marks the end of the historical, human Savior. It seems all four Gospels tell the same story; Jesus came to die. More detail is given surrounding Jesus' arrest, trial, beatings, and crucifixion, than any of His works, His healings and miracles.

You might say the whole purpose of His life was to die. No biography of any person would give greater details and explanation to their means of death than the formation of their beliefs and their life's accomplishments. Although Jesus rose from the dead, still more detail is given to His sufferings and death than His coming back to life. Greater detail is given to His arrest, beatings, whipping, crown of thorns, robe, carrying His own cross, nailing to the cross, the sign above His head, and His seven sayings from the cross. In fact, several chapters are dedicated to the details of this one event. More than any specific healing or miracle that occupy only a few verses of a chapter.

After this one dramatic event of His crucifixion, death, and resurrection, He remained on earth with His disciples. For forty days He showed Himself to a few at a time or before one great crowd to prove He was alive and had risen from the dead. During these forty days, He did not preach another sermon, perform another miracle, or heal any person. Then He ascended to heaven and was seated until He will return for the Church and later to rule the earth. The obvious question we ask is WHY?

JESUS' DEATH WAS THE INTRODUCTION TO THE MAIN MESSAGE

Jesus' death and sudden departure only set the stage for the main message, the main act, the coming of the Church, His body. Act one was Jesus' life and death on earth. The forty days after His resurrection was the intermission. Then the second and greatest act is the coming of Christ's body. Out of His death came our life, *"Christ in you the hope of glory."* The Head had to go to heaven so the body could be formed, filled with His same life, and anointed by the same Holy Spirit power and authority.

During His earthly ministry, Jesus preached God's message and was God's ambassador. The next sermon after Jesus' last sermon was Peter's sermon on the Day of Pentecost. Now *we* have been given God's message and are God's ambassadors (2 Corinthians 5:17-20). This message and ministry were given to His Church forty days after His ascension on the Day of Pentecost. God's desire was to replace His only Son with a multitude of sons and daughters.

Jesus who said, *"I am the light,"* had that light extinguished at His death. Now His light has been reignited in us. He told His disciples, *"you are the light of the world."* Jesus, who also said, *"I am the life,"* saw that life killed on the cross. Now His eternal life has been given to anyone who will believe. He says to us, *"My life I give to you,"* and *"Anyone who believes in me will never die."*

WE ARE NOT ONLY MEMBERS WITH GOD, BUT MEMBERS WITH EACH OTHER

If you are going blind, your nose cannot fill the place of the eye. If the heart is failing, the stomach cannot fill in and pump blood. Each part of our body plays a unique role as each of us do in the body of Christ.

We are as much one with each other as we are one with Christ and God the Father. God does not see us as Baptists, Methodists, or Pentecostals—He sees us as Christ's One Body. If you are born again, you are a member of the body of Christ, one with the Father, Jesus

Christ, and all other believers. The only one who is not part of the body of Christ is the one who does not believe in the work of Jesus as the only way to heaven.

Without Jesus in our life, we can have no fellowship with God in life, and we will have no fellowship with God in eternity. We can have no fellowship with each other in life and no fellowship with each other in eternity.

When a radical Muslim beheads a Christian, he does not ask if he is Baptist, Methodist or Catholic. He thinks we are all Christians. WHY CAN'T WE?

Sadly, we not only see ourselves separate from other denominations but also separate from each other, those of our own church group or fellowship. We separate from our own over the rapture, confession of sins (1 John 1:9), or whether or not we can lose our salvation. ONLY faith in Jesus makes us Christians, members of the body of Christ, and sends us to heaven. Not whether we are Spirit filled, believe in the rapture, or confession of sins. When God sees us, He sees hands, feet, ears, and eyes. When He sees us, He sees Christ. SO SHOULD WE.

> *Now John answered Him, saying, "Teacher, we saw someone who does not follow us casting out demons in Your name, and we forbade him because he does not follow us."*
>
> *But Jesus said, "Do not forbid him, for no one who works a miracle in My name can soon afterward*

speak evil of Me. For he who is not against us is on our side" (Mark 9:38-40).

If two Christians arrived in heaven at the same time, one Spirit-filled and the other not, Jesus would receive both with the same joy. There is no such thing as a Baptist ear and a Methodist nose or a Presbyterian foot and an Assembly of God eye. We are part of Christ's body only because we are born again.

We may not agree on every doctrine, but we are each part of the body of Christ. We all have a mission to the world, and we are all going to heaven. I am connected to you, you are connected to me, and we are both connected to Christ. We all need each other.

Chapter 14

OUR UNIQUE PLACE IN THE BODY OF CHRIST

If the foot should say, "Because I am not a hand, I am not of the body," is it therefore not of the body? And if the ear should say, "Because I am not an eye, I am not of the body," is it therefore not of the body? If the whole body were an eye where would be the hearing? If the whole were hearing, where would be the smelling? But now God has set the members, each one of them, in the body just as He pleased (1 Corinthians 12:15-18).

It is not often we find such a large passage of scripture emphasizing the sovereignty of each member of the Godhead. But in 1 Corinthians 12 the entire chapter deals with God's wisdom surpassing ours. In verse 11, we are told that the Holy Spirit divides the spiritual gifts into our lives *"as He wills."* In verse 18, we are told that

God the Father places us in the body of Christ *"just as He pleased."*

In other words, for us to change places with another minister we admire would be as difficult as the foot trading places with the hand and the ear trading places with the eye. Not only is it impossible to do, but it is also impossible for one part to take the place of another. You cannot successfully walk with your hands and you cannot see through your ear. We are unique in our position and function in the Body of Christ.

THE INFINITE IMAGINATION OF GOD

Snowflakes

I stay in many hotels when I travel to both large and small cities. In one small town, I stayed at the only hotel. I was surprised, when I turned on the television to find only a few stations available and a national selection almost nonexistent. I ended up watching the Weather Channel. That's how desperate I was just to see something. To my surprise, they had an interesting one-hour special on snowflakes. The program confirmed what was thought to be true for decades—no two snowflakes are the same. This could not be proven for years, because accurate pictures of each flake seemed impossible.

A serious effort began in the 1970s to take pictures of snowflakes at night with the blackness of the night behind each flake. The flash of the light bulbs caused just enough heat to melt the outside edges of the flakes, so no accurate pictures could be taken. But in the 1990s, LED bulbs were created making light without heat, and the most incredible pictures were taken of snowflakes world-wide by cooperating international meteorologists.

It was found that the consistency of snow was different at various locations. The snow was different in makeup on the east side of the Rockies than on the west side. Snow was different in the U.S. northwest, central plains, and northeast. Snow was different in consistency in Canada, the Himalayas, the Andes, and the Pyrenees. And it was now concluded with great proof, no two snowflakes were the same, anywhere, out of the trillions falling each day. This led to the conclusion that no two snowflakes had ever or would ever be the same. Each snowflake is individual and unique. Oh, the infinite imagination of God.

Animals

No two animals, fish, or birds are the same. Even dogs or cats from the same litter are different sizes, have unique markings, and personalities. So it is with every species of animals, birds, fish, and plants.

Flowers

Andrew Womack told a story about how he and his wife Jamie went walking alone into one of the highest regions of the Rocky Mountains. They came across a valley covered with millions of yellow flowers as far as the eye could see. The flowers came up to their waist and they walked through them like a scene from a movie, with their hands touching the tops of them. They walked quite a distance back to their hotel room and looked up the flowers and found they grow only in that valley and bloom one week out of the year. They happened to be there and saw no one else in the area.

Andrew questioned God as to why He would make such a beautiful flower, then let it bloom for one week without caring if anyone saw it. He said the Lord spoke to him and told him He made it for Himself and doesn't need anyone else's approval. Revelation 4:11 (KJV) says, *"Thou hast created all things, and for thy pleasure they are and were created."*

THE UNIVERSE

Stars

No two stars are the same size, brightness, color, or have the same chemical composition.

Planets

Like stars, no two planets are the same size or have the same composition of rock, soil or atmosphere. No two are the same color or brightness.

Moons

For years, we here on earth looking at the planets with our large telescopes saw only two or three moons orbiting the planets closest to the earth. But with our new telescopes placed in outer space and our probes sent to a few of these planets, we discovered Jupiter has seventy-nine moons and Saturn has eighty-two. And you guessed it, no two moons are alike. They are unique moons, orbiting unique planets throughout the universe. We had to throw away many sets of encyclopedias with their outdated information.

No one but angels see the stars and planets as they travel the universe from heaven to earth and back, to deliver divine answers for the children of God. God doesn't care if He has an audience to see His works. He needs no approval.

Our One Moon

Our moon is uniquely for our planet earth. The moon held our imaginations for over 6,000 years because no one could get close enough to study it. Was it made of cheese? Could we live there? What was on the dark side?

In July 1969 we went to the moon and discovered the dark and unseen side looks like the visible side. The moon is not fit for human life. It has no atmosphere and has too little gravity. It is too hot to exist on the visible side and too cold on the dark side. To remain alive, we had to take our own air, water, and food.

We can't live there because we don't belong there. Each astronaut's home could be seen over their shoulder on the horizon. If there were lunar beings, they would be as much out of place on earth as we were on the moon.

After six thousand years, we found the moon to be just a big rock covered with dust.

YOU ALSO ARE UNIQUE

You Are One of a Kind in Your Physical Birth

> *He has made from one blood every nation of men to dwell on all the face of the earth, and has determined the preappointed times and boundaries of their dwellings* (Acts 17:26).

Like our place in the body of Christ, and our spiritual gifts given by the Holy Spirit, everything concerning our physical birth is unique and part of God's sovereignty.

A great contentment is found in accepting yourself as God has made you. Your birth time, continent, country, and city of birth were pre-chosen by God. Your socio-economic environment, nationality, color, gender, parents, personality, and looks are uniquely yours.

Your personal identity is unique. Your DNA, retinas, and voice print can all be used to identify you from everyone else on the earth. Also, your ten unique fingerprints were developed in the womb at the same time your ten unique toe prints were being formed. We use our fingerprints for identification, but do not consider that our toe prints are just as unique. No one else has these exact qualities, never has, and never will. God just smiles.

Each of us have individual quirks. One afternoon, I was in a restaurant with a minister and I sneezed. My sister walked from across the dining room and told me she heard me sneeze and said, "I recognize that sneeze, that's my brother."

God broke the mold with you even if you're an identical twin. Your mother knows the difference. God did not make you a duplication, but a separate creation. You continue to be unique in life, in marriage, in your desires, and how you work in your occupation and accomplish goals.

Children all have different desires. Instead of trying to steer your children into the same career you have chosen, or into an occupation that will bring them a good income, turn them loose and let them follow their dreams. The old saying is true for your children too, "If you love what you do, you'll never work a day in your life."

You Are Further Unique as a Christian

> *When it pleased God, who separated me from my mother's womb and called me through His grace, to reveal His Son in me, that I might preach Him among the Gentiles...* (Galatians 1:15-16).

Further separation occurs at the new birth as you enter into a new life and your own calling. Though others have the same gifts of the Holy Spirit and are called into the same office, you are unique in how you handle these gifts from God. How you teach, share, or witness is unique to you. I am convinced that if every pastor in a city preached from the same passage on Easter Sunday morning, no two ministers would preach the passage the same way.

God may even place a life location into your calling.

After pastoring, Loretta and I thought we would like to move to Southern California. I was no longer employed by the church and could travel from any airport to conduct my ministry. Despite the cost of living, we thought we could afford a nice apartment and keep our existing home in Tulsa. We found a place and then returned to Tulsa to examine our financial situation and decided to buy it. When we called back to purchase the apartment, it was sold and so was every other unit.

We flew out again to California the next year determined to find a place to live and found nothing we liked. We flew back to Tulsa and as we were landing, we looked at each other and said, "Tulsa is our home." We realized it was part of our DNA. We can vacation in California, but we will never live there.

Location bases existed in the Old and New Testament.

Gilgal was the home location to return to by the Israelites when they fought the wars in Canaan. After each battle, the people returned to Gilgal. Jerusalem was home base after the Day of Pentecost to take the gospel into the Jewish world and back. Antioch was set up by the Lord for Paul and his teams to take the gospel into the Gentile world and back.

You have a home base too. I speak to many Bible school students and usually warn them on the first day, "Don't think God will never send you back to your hometown. You may not want to go back because the people know you and your old way of life. You may be relieved you are gone, but God may have you return. Who else could show the grace of God to those you grew up with?"

You Will Still Be Unique Into Eternity

> *There is one glory of the sun, another glory of the moon, and another glory of the stars; for one star differs from another star in glory. So also is the resurrection of the dead. The body is sown in corruption, it is raised in incorruption* (1 Corinthians 15:41-42).

Going to heaven is not a reward but a gift. Anyone who accepts Jesus will be in heaven. We go to heaven because of our faith in Jesus, but our rewards will be based on our works we did after receiving Jesus (Revelation 14:13). Our individuality will be seen in the rewards we will all receive for our service on earth during the time between our salvation and our departure to heaven.

No two Christians will be rewarded the same in eternity. Just like every planet and star is different in brightness in the heavens, so will we be. We will be as different in heaven in our eternal reign with Christ as we were in this life with our unique birth and individual positions and gifts.

We will not be rewarded in life or later in heaven by an amount of production, but by our faithfulness and ability with what we were given. The same thing will be said to the steward who had five talents as the one who had ten, *"Well done, good and faithful servant. You have been faithful over a few things; I will make you ruler over many things..."* (Matthew 25:20-23). Jesus further clarified this, *"...to whom much is given, from him much will be required..."* (Luke 12:48).

THE FOLLY OF ENVYING OTHER MINISTERS AND CHURCHES

So, in your personal ministry why do you spend your life looking at others in wonder and envy? It is alright to learn from others in the ministry, but don't try to imitate them. When I taught at Rhema Bible Training Center, I saw many students trying to imitate the founder, Kenneth Hagin. They seemed to think if they spoke like him and used his mannerisms in the pulpit, they would end up as successful as him.

Your success really begins when you learn to be yourself. If God would have wanted you to be someone else, He would have made two of you. He broke the mold when He made you. Honor God's choice in making you the way you are and let the real you out. Your ministry on earth will be as unique as your position and rewards in heaven.

Pastors of small churches usually want to swap for larger ones. Pastors of large churches often want to swap for smaller ones. If you could swap places with another, you would find their life call was just a big rock covered with dust. You could not exist in their ministry. You left your home behind you. Their call works for them but not for anyone else, especially you. We look at each other in envy instead of seeing the only one who needs to appreciate us is us. The only one who can handle and understand your world is you. So appreciate it.

You are a unique blend of personality, vision, gifts, and ministry call. Your happiness is not over there, but right here, where you are located and in your heart. You could travel a long way to be someone else and then fail. Nothing is worth quitting your call, then regretting it. Stop searching for what does not exist. So on which side is the grass greener? *Yours.*

Chapter 15

SINS OF IMMATURITY

In a great house there are not only vessels of gold and silver, but also of wood and clay, some for honor and some for dishonor. Therefore if anyone cleanses himself from the latter, he will be a vessel for honor, sanctified and useful for the Master, prepared for every good work. Flee also youthful lusts; but pursue righteousness, faith, love, peace with those who call on the Lord out of a pure heart. But avoid foolish and ignorant disputes, knowing that they generate strife (2 Timothy 2:20-23).

EVERY BOOK OF THE BIBLE IS FOR EVERY BELIEVER

Although we identify certain books of the New Testament as pastoral epistles, every book of the New Testament, and Old Testament for that matter, are for all believers. Paul told Timothy, *"All scripture is given by inspiration of*

God and is profitable...that the man of God may be complete [mature], *thoroughly equipped for every good work*" (2 Timothy 3:16-17). If you try to make certain books only for certain individuals, pastors, teachers, etc. you would have to go further and say that one book is only for Christians living in Rome or Galatia or Ephesus. *All scripture* means *all scripture.*

It can be taken also that all scripture is meant for pulpit ministers too. You can't declare yourself above living righteously because you are divinely set in a ministry position over the congregation. Godliness is profitable for all believers, including those called into full-time ministry, those deriving their income from preaching and teaching the Word of God to others. So I say it again, all scripture is meant for all believers.

ALSO

The key word found in our passage we will be studying from 2 Timothy 2 is the word "also" found in verse 22, *"Flee also youthful lusts...."* Not only is the congregation to flee youthful lusts, so *also* is the pastor. A better definition of *"youthful lusts"* is sins of immaturity. Sins of thoughts and actions are warned of in the Old and New Testament. Unlike David who fell into adultery, Joseph ran from the sin. We also, like Joseph, are told to *"flee fornication"*—to run from it (1 Corinthians 6:18 KJV). Now we are warned in the same manner, along with Timothy, to *flee* or run from youthful lusts, sins of immaturity.

Paul is telling Timothy that running from sinful lusts is not just for the congregation, but for the minister as well. There are no separate rules toward sin for the clergy than the congregation. God will judge ministers by a higher standard than He does other believers when we all stand before the Judgment Seat of Christ (James 3:1). Iniquity is iniquity and righteousness is righteousness. Even Jesus was judged in His earthly life by this standard. When He sat down at the right hand of God, after completing His earthly ministry, the Father said to Him, *"You have loved righteousness and hated lawlessness* [iniquity]..." (Hebrews 1:9). That is a great rule to govern our own lives by.

THE MINISTER AND SINS OF IMMATURITY

Yet, according to the instructions given to Timothy by Paul, there are certain sins associated with ministers in their youth, or immaturity. All sins of immaturity are associated with arrogance. Sadly, it is true that many young ministers think they have found answers no one else has found or even thought of. They can't wait to enter the pulpit to prove to their local church, and also the vast number of other ministers, that their ideas are what everyone has been waiting for.

But when the same problems occur with their ministry that occur within other ministries, they become confused. Instead of opening up to the possibility they may have been wrong, they dig in their heels and become obstinate, fighting for a lost cause. Sadly, not only do seasoned ministers recognize their wrong attitude, so do the members of the congregation. People leave and the minister ends up blaming the people, not his own blindness. It has been said, "Arrogance is the only disease that makes everyone sick except the one who has it."

I want to address certain sins of immaturity I have observed and recorded that are found in the pulpit today. This is certainly not an exhaustive list but should cover enough to help ministers recognize they are not alone in their wrong attitudes and also in the answers to them.

SINS OF IMMATURITY INCLUDE:

1. You are driven by attendance numbers.

Joy and sadness are not only driven by things we see but by decisions we make about what we see. If you are the pastor of a church, you need to be content with those who show up. Quit preaching to the empty seats and preach to the full ones—to those who got up, showered, dressed themselves and their children and made it to the church. And quit preaching to the ones who came about those who did not come. Show your gratitude to those who came and perhaps they will ask others to come.

Most church attendance is increased by happy church attenders who invite others to find the fulfillment they have found in the church. If you take credit for those who come, you will also feel responsible for those who leave. Acts 2:47 tells us that *"the Lord added to the church daily those who were being saved.*" I'm not saying we should leave it all to the Lord and not invite people to church. But the drawing of the Holy Spirit and the joy of the Lord should witness to the visitors they have found the right church and should continue attending.

2. You must have the largest church in the city.

Not everyone is called to pastor a large church. Even the churches of the book of Acts were different sizes. And not all large churches preach and teach the Word of God. Many churches are large because of their youth, children, or worship ministry. I would rather see a city with many smaller churches that preach the Word of God than one or two large churches built on programs. Numbers of people attending do not indicate success.

Jesus purposely tested the crowds with difficult statements to weed out those who did not want to truly follow Him and grow in the Christian life. On one occasion, when Jesus challenged the multitudes with a difficult spiritual choice, they all left. Jesus did not get upset or look for a "group hug" from His disciples. He asked them if they too wanted to leave (John 6:53-68).

3. Each sermon must outdo the last.

You are not called to compete with the church down the street. But you are also not called to compete with yourself. When we preach a sermon that has everyone saying "amen" and shouting for joy, we often feel compelled to make the next sermon even better. Your standard for the next sermon should not be the quality of the one you just preached. You obeyed God's voice and preached the sermon God led you to preach. Jesus told the crowds He did the works and spoke the words of His Father (John 8:28,38; 10:37). Your only source of contentment after the word is preached, is the assurance you preached what God instructed you to preach.

4. You look for compliments to judge the quality of your sermon.

This is close to the previous point in its application. Your stamp of approval is not the compliments, or lack of, from your congregation. Most who tell you the sermon was good are lying. They did not like the message but would never tell you so. They see you coming down the aisle and say, "Good sermon, Pastor." You would say the same thing to another minister. The only compliment you need is the peace in your heart you preached the sermon God told you to preach. He will never lie to you. So quit being too moved by compliments and criticism. You are never going to be loved by everyone. But you are always loved by God.

5. You preach to impress other ministers.

When you really preach a sermon that you know came from God, even receiving revelation while you preached, you not only want all the congregation to take a copy of the message home but wish they would share it with a notable minister in town. Not only that, but they may also share it with a notable national minister. You feel, somehow, your sermons must be heard by those you consider leaders in your area or even the nation.

It is true that most ministers who are invited to speak at a minister's conference do not speak to the needs of the registrants present, but to impress the other speakers sitting on the front row. They hope to be invited to their church someday. It is not up to you to spread your fame—it is up to God. Jesus did not try to make His fame increase but preached and healed in obedience to His Father. "... *Then His fame went throughout all Syria...*" (Matthew 4:23-24).

6. You preach your own view on subjects to distance yourself doctrinally from the group your church came from.

Your church might have come out of a denomination, a spiritual movement, or a specific doctrinal background. You might have come from the Assemblies of God, the Word of Faith, or the teaching of Grace. You have a disagreement with certain parts of these beliefs, so you distance yourself completely from it. You end up splintering and fracturing the congregation.

When those issues come up in a sermon, tread lightly and walk in love. You may think some people treat grace as a license to sin. You may think some ministers use the message of prosperity to just get money from others. When you come to a passage, preach on it in love and in balance. Teach the truth on the subject and approach the excesses with an abundance of compassion and scriptures. Most of your congregation will thank you.

7. You speak to reach certain age groups, colors, or demographics.

There are many things you can do to draw in a group but don't preach to draw segments of society you are trying to reach. Fill positions of greeters, ushers, or praise and worship leaders with a variety of faithful and spiritual attenders. Let your last priority be to choose young, middle-aged, and old including all races and nationalities. What people see when they enter makes an impression, that in this church *anyone who loves God and people can be used by God*. But the Word of God itself is without age, color, or nationality. The Word and the preaching should be for everyone. So just be you when you preach. You have a style that is unique. Use it and don't try to draw a certain group of people using someone else's style. Just be yourself and preach to whoever walks in.

8. You focus your attention on those who do not or will not grow.

In our opening passage, 2 Timothy 2:22, Paul told Timothy to *"pursue righteousness, faith, love, and peace with those who call on the Lord out of a pure heart."* In other words, if you want to maintain your joy, be encouraged, and know your ministry is doing well; when you preach keep your eyes on those who are strong in prayer, *"call on the Lord,"* and maintain a life of purity *"out of a pure heart."*

Keep scattering the seed, preaching the Word, and stop looking at those who have a blank or angry look. Quit wondering when they will ever get the importance of the Word and keep your eyes on those who do get it. These are the ones with a big smile, and at times shout an encouraging, "Amen!"

Chapter 16

Ten Things I Wish I Had Been Taught in Bible College

A Bible college or theology class cannot teach you everything you need to know about the daily church and personal life situations of the pastor and those who attend. These have to be lived out and experienced. This is also why it is important while you attend a Bible college that you become involved in a local church. You put to work in the church what you learn in school. You also take what you learn in the church and apply it to your training in school. Even the best Bible colleges are not a church and are no substitute for a church.

This is why you will have fewer troubles with these "ten things" if you realize what you learn in church while attending school may at times be more important than what you get from a book or lecturer.

I am an instructor at Andrew Wommack's ministry training school, Charis Bible College. These ten observations came from alumni who are now pastoring:

1. BASIC LEADERSHIP SKILLS

"I wish someone would have taught me basic leadership skills. I was well grounded in theology and Bible exegesis, but seminary did not prepare me for the real world of real people. It would have been great to have someone walk alongside me before my first church."

This is why, during Bible school or even after Bible school, it is good to work with a pastor. Quit waiting for a minister to walk alongside of you and find one you can walk with. Theology and sermon preparation can be taught, but how to work with people can only be learned by working with people. Timothy found this out, even after long travels learning beside Paul. Both books to Timothy were more about dealing with people than putting sermons together. Paul might have taught a few human issues to his team, but no two people or people problems are the same. They just have to be experienced and handled as well as possible. What is necessary for handling people is a heart of love and a head full of spiritual common sense.

This was seen when two women were fighting over possession of a child before King Solomon. When he said to cut the baby in half and give one half to each woman, the true mother cried out to let the other woman have the child. This is spiritual brilliance.

Paul commended the pastor at Colosse, Epaphras, and called him *"one of you"* (Colossians 1:7-8, 4:12-13). He was probably saved in the church and came up through the church learning both doctrine, sermon preparation, and how to handle people.

2. PERSONAL FINANCIAL ISSUES

"I needed to know a lot more about personal financial issues. No one ever told me about minister's housing, social security, automobile reimbursement, and the difference between a package and a salary. I got burned in my first church."

You cannot be taught everything in Bible school, and you don't have to be. This is why you depend on good people in the secular market—CPAs, bankers, and tax advisors. Or you can put faithful, knowledgeable people in your church on the board to keep you and all the other board members on track and informed. Every good leader seeks help for the people he oversees. God has not called to you minister to everyone, but to see to it everyone is ministered to.

3. DEALING WITH POWER PEOPLE

"I wish I had been given advice on how to deal with power groups and power people in the church. I got it all wrong in my first two churches. I was fired outright from the first

church and pressured out in the second one. Someone finally and courageously pointed out how I was messing things up almost from the moment I began in a new church. I am so thankful that I am in the ninth year of a happy pastorate in my third church."

Moses had opposition from power people—his own brother and sister, Aaron and Miriam. They opposed his leadership over Israel even telling each other they could run the nation as well as Moses (Numbers 12:2). David was betrayed by Ahithophel, Jesus by Judas, and Paul by many close to him. You can only learn by living through this. It is difficult to teach.

One man in my church came to me after I had been appointed pastor and told me he was more qualified to take the church. He told me he could preach better sermons, knew more Greek and Hebrew than I did, and could handle church business better than me. In other words, he was angry and thought he should have been pastor, instead of me. I told him I agreed with everything he said. I had very little Greek and no Hebrew at all, and I had to bring in those for counsel who understood business. I told him there was only one difference between me and him, I was called.

I found through the years that those who argue continually over the same issues are not just being antagonistic. The subject of their disagreement is not the real issue. The issue is control. This can only be recognized and learned by dealing with controlling people. One woman tried to control Jesus by asking Him to put her two sons on each side of Him in His upcoming kingdom (Matthew 20:20-21). People and times have not changed when it comes to personal ambition.

4. PERSONAL PRAYER AND STUDY

"Don't give up your time in prayer and the Word. I really don't ever remember anyone pointing me in that direction. The busier I became at the church, the more I neglected my primary calling. It was a subtle process; I wish I had been forewarned."

Billy Graham was interviewed late in his life by Larry King. Reverend Graham was asked what his greatest regret was in his ministry. He answered by saying he wished he would have spent more time in study and prayer for his personal life than just for sermon preparation. This can become an occupational hazard in a minister's life. It is easy to read a good doctrinal book or listen to a sermon and think, "That is a good point. I must make a sermon out of it." The first thought should be to use it in your personal life and increase your worship, love, and appreciation toward God.

Most of the mistakes I have made in preaching was more of a lack of prayer than study and preparation. Too often I have under-prayed and over-studied. Prayer gives the spiritual sensitivity to know during the sermon, what to mention and what to leave out.

This too cannot be taught. This is a personal commitment to prayer, to seek first the kingdom of God and His righteousness.

5. Understanding Business

"I wish someone would have told me I needed some business training. I felt inadequate and embarrassed in the first budget meetings. And it really hit home when we looked at a building program that involved fundraising and debt. I had no clue what the bankers were saying."

You don't have to have more business training. God does not require anything outside of a call to the ministry, an honest report inside and outside the church, being filled with the Holy Spirit, and being filled with the wisdom of the Word. You are you, and do not have to be trained in natural skills, such as business principles. Go with your strengths and bring in others to fill in for your weaknesses. You are the boss so quit feeling inadequate, the dumb one. You will pick up the knowledge needed by being present in business meetings yet to come. Also, don't be afraid to tell the bank presidents and CPAs to speak slowly and explain. You are no more a banker than they are a pastor. And there are no stupid questions. Someone else sitting at the board table will probably thank you for asking the same question they were afraid to ask for fear of looking stupid.

6. MEAN PEOPLE

"Someone should have told me that there are mean people in the church. Look, I was prepared to deal with critics. That is a reality of any leadership position. But I never expected a few of the members to be so mean and cruel. One church member wrote something really cruel on my Facebook wall. Both my wife and children cried when they read it."

You can't stop people from being mean, but you can minimize it by teaching about it in your sermons. Teach from the Word, including the Sermon on the Mount and Proverbs, how to handle anger and disagreements. Tell your people if they have a disagreement with you, come and talk to you. If someone in the church comes to them with a gripe about someone, ask them if they have spoken to the person. The word says, *"If you have something against your brother, go to him"* (Matthew 5:23-24, 18:15). If you won't, then "don't bring it to me." You might also add that if they won't go to the person they are speaking of, you will arrange the meeting between them so they can sit together and work it out according to the Word. This really stops a lot of future contention.

7. MAINTAINING A NORMAL FAMILY

"Show me how to help my kids grow up like normal kids. I really worry about the glass house syndrome with my wife and kids. I'm particularly worried that my children will see so much of the negative that they will grow up hating the church. I've seen it happen too many times."

Be real with your kids about people, sinners and saints. And also be real with them about themselves. They are no different from anyone else. They do not have to live in a fishbowl and be constantly on guard. They did not choose to be born into a minister's family. They do not have to end up as a minister in the church no matter what the members of the congregation think. Because you are a pastor or on staff in a church doesn't mean your children have to be.

Your children should grow up to hear God's call and will for themselves. They, nor you, chose this calling. God called you and He will take care of your children and those who put undue pressure on your children. Tell your children to relax. It is the people who have a problem, not them.

8. MAINTAINING A STRONG MARRIAGE

"I wish I had been told to continue to date my wife. I was diligent in dating my wife before I became a pastor. I then got so busy helping others with their needs that I neglected her. I almost lost my marriage. She felt so alone as I tried to meet everyone's needs but hers."

Don't let the church become the "other woman." Your wife can't slap a church like she can a flirting woman. You had your wife before you pastored, and you will still have her after you step down. This position is temporary, but your marriage is not. Wives and children do not become discouraged because you have to break your plans for a sudden death or emergency in the church. They can understand this. They become discouraged when you do not reschedule the plans. They will keep their confidence in you when they know you have and always will keep them at a level of preeminence in your personal life.

9. YOU CAN ONLY BE IN ONE PLACE AT A TIME

"Someone needed to tell me about the expectation of being omnipresent. I had no idea that people would expect me to be at so many meetings, so many church socials, and so many sports and civic functions. It is impossible to meet all those expectations, so I left some folks disappointed or angry."

Tell the congregation in a church service or open meeting that you are human, not Superman or God Himself. In the service or at the office, you are their pastor. After that, your family is most important. You will attend the events you choose, not those they choose for you. You will take vacations and times off. You will benefit them more if you are refreshed. They take vacations and time off. You are just as human as they are. If it relaxes and refreshes them, it will do the same for you and your family.

10. DEALING WITH DYING PEOPLE

"I really needed help knowing how to minister to dying people. Some of those who have terminal illnesses have such a strong faith that they minister to me. But many of them are scared and have questions I never anticipated. I was totally

unprepared for these pastoral care issues when I first became a pastor."

Church members dying and having funerals and memorial services are normal. Every minister had to begin somewhere. I recommend you make friends with seasoned pastors in your city or other pastor friends you can contact by phone. There are good books available on weddings, terminal illness, and funeral etiquette. You can also download sermons and find special service outlines online. This profession is thousands of years old and every minister out there has run into the same problems you are facing. There is nothing new under the sun.

ABOUT THE AUTHOR

For more than 40 years Bob Yandian has taught the unchanging truth of God's Word. He pastored Grace Fellowship in Tulsa, Oklahoma for 33 years where he raised up and sent out hundreds of ministers to churches and missions organizations around the world through the School of the Local Church, and Grace School of Ministry.

Bob's mission is to train up a new generation in the Word of God through his *Student of the Word* broadcast, and by ministering in Bible schools, minister's conferences, and churches.

Known as an expositor of the Bible, he is widely acknowledged as one of the most knowledgeable teachers of this generation. His practical insight and wisdom into the Word of God has helped countless people to grow to maturity in the Christian life.

Bob is a graduate of Trinity Bible College where he studied under Charles Duncomb, an associate of Smith Wigglesworth. He served as both instructor and Dean of Instructors at Rhema Bible Training Center. Pastor Yandian serves on the board of Joyce Meyer Ministries, and Andrew Wommack Ministries.

OUR VISION

Proclaiming the truth and the power of the Gospel of Jesus Christ with excellence. Challenging Christians to live victoriously, grow spiritually, know God intimately.

Connect with us on

 Facebook @ HarrisonHousePublishers

and Instagram @ HarrisonHousePublishing

so you can stay up to date with news

about our books and our authors.

Visit us at **www.harrisonhouse.com**

for a complete product listing as well as

monthly specials for wholesale distribution.